Soaring
HOPE

*Imagining Life As
It Ought To Be*

LYNN THRUSH

Presented To:

_____

From:

_____

Date:

_____

Soaring
HOPE

DESTINY IMAGE₀ PUBLISHERS, INC.
P.O. Box 310, Shippensburg, PA 17257-0310
"Promoting Inspired Lives."

This book and all other Destiny Image, Revival Press, Mercy-Place, Fresh Bread, Destiny Image Fiction, and Treasure House books are available at Christian bookstores and distributors worldwide.

For a U.S. bookstore nearest you, call 1-800-722-6774.
For more information on foreign distributors, call 717-532-3040.
Reach us on the Internet: www.destinyimage.com.

ISBN 13 TP: 978-0-7684-0310-7
ISBN 13 Ebook: 978-0-7684-8776-3

For Worldwide Distribution, Printed in the U.S.A.
1 2 3 4 5 6 7 8 / 16 15 14 13 12

DEDICATION

To: Carol
Sharing hopefulness with you over a long time is a gracious and sacred privilege.

To: Alan, Beth, Michael, Emily, and Sheena
I see you investing in hopeful enterprises—how powerful.

To: Simon and Nadia
I never expected to be a grandpa; now, enthusiastically, I say, "Your future is bright."

Acknowledgments

I acknowledge four distant mentors whose insights and spirits have paved the way for me to enter the delights of the good news of God.

Desmond Ford, a Seventh-Day Adventist theologian who helped me to interpret and then love the prophetic literature of the Bible.

David and Karen Mains, who helped me appreciate the significance of the local church.

Ralph Winter, who so creatively called the Church to take the good news to all the world.

N.T. Wright, who continues to elevate Jesus as the true God of the world.

ENDORSEMENTS

Christians will never change the world, Lynn Thrush contends, apart from hope and imagination. But hope and imagination suffer when private morality trumps the common good and when the life to come obscures the life we live today. In this powerful, practical, and intensely constructive book, Thrush guides us into a deeper, richer, and more faithful understanding of the biblical text—an understanding that can liberate Christians for the world-transforming work that God has called us to undertake.

RICHARD T. HUGHES
Director, Sider Institute for Anabaptist, Pietist, and Wesleyan Studies at Messiah College
Author, *Christian America and the Kingdom of God*

Frankly, the constant moaning about how bad things are really gets old. Of all people, Christians should be the harbingers of optimism and hope. Lynn Thrush, in this book, invites you to embrace the heart of the Christian message and find the hope it brings to everyone. He challenges us to think differently about our language, our mental constructs, our tendency to bemoan a loss of influence, and to soar with the energy, optimism, joy, and possibilities that come with truly bringing the Kingdom of God near. The natural human spiral into despair is soundly reversed in *Soaring Hope: Imagining Life As It Ought To Be*. Catch a vision of God's idea of life for you!

KEVIN W. MANNOIA, PhD
Chaplain, Azusa Pacific University
Founder and Chair, Wesleyan Holiness Consortium
Former President, National Association of Evangelicals

Lynn Thrush has a "deeply hopeful" understanding of God's will for the world as revealed in the Bible. Too often people—including Christians—become locked into a hopeless view of life and the future, sometimes appealing to the Bible in rationalizing their hopelessness. On the contrary, Thrush finds story after story in the Bible that gives people reason to hope here-and-now for the improvement of their lives and world as well as hope for eternal life.

DON THORSEN, PhD
Professor of Theology, Chair of Graduate Department of
Theology and Ethics
Azusa Pacific University

I commend this book to every Christian in every corner of the world. Here is a book that will change your thinking and understanding of what it means to live with hope in a hopeless world. Like pieces of cloth neatly put together to form a magnificent quilt, Scriptures and ideas have been brought together to make sense of life and yet challenge our long-seated belief in the future we long to embrace. In going through the pages of this book real hope is rekindled. Life is worth living and the future worth pursuing.

There is a silent cry within many hearts for something better and more meaningful in life. For this very reason this book is timely. When we know our sovereign God is in control, God's people are also in control—they possess the land! When God is in charge, Christians are in control and secure in His might.

God's people, wherever they are around the world are an embodiment of hope! They are the bearers of the good news. They are the messengers of hope. The rest of humankind ought to be drawn to them, to feed and experience what the world has from the beginning desired and promised to give, yet without success—hope.

Hope oils the engine of our lives so that the engine keeps working. It creates overcomers out of those overcome by hopelessness. Hope has power to bring wholeness to situations and circumstances of life where otherwise disintegration and disillusionment about life seem to prevail. One is better off reading this book than ignoring it!

Danisa Ndlovu
Bishop, Brethren in Christ Church of Zimbabwe
President, Mennonite World Conference
Zimbabwe, Africa

CONTENTS

FOREWORD

IF THERE IS A DEFAULT setting in contemporary Christianity, it is unquestionably that of fatalism.

Having lived through the end of the world one more time this past year, predicted by a well-meaning, yet thoroughly uninformed follower of Jesus Christ (I forget how many of these predictions I have lived through in my lifetime), I was beginning to wonder if I was the only one longing for an alternative way of reading the Bible and responding to the world.

Then, along comes Lynn Thrush with his book, *Soaring Hope: Imagining Life As It Ought To Be.* Now I know that I am not alone.

In this provocative work, the author dares to ask counter-culture questions like: What if this world is not something to escape, but something to renew? What if the God of Abraham still desires to bless the entire world?

What if this God is not only God of the "sweet bye and bye," but also God of the here and now?

What if the good news is actually good enough to help restore an evil and broken world?

The author grew up under the achingly negative teaching he critiques. This largely dispensational view of the Bible was not intended to be overly pessimistic; it sincerely desired to be true to the witness of Scripture. Yet, as Thrush argues compellingly, this view of the Bible and the world is not sufficiently rooted in the Scriptures themselves, and falls uncomfortably short of adequately describing God's irrepressible hope for the world.

This book takes as its starting place the life and teachings of Jesus. Christ's prayer for God's Kingdom to come and will to be done on earth as it is in Heaven (see Matt. 6:10) is ground zero for Thrush's theological paradigm. The practical outworking of his interpretation of Scripture is the Incarnation itself. Christ taking on human flesh is God's most affirming statement about the state of the world; it is a world worth redeeming, and the incarnate Christ is the fulfillment of God's grand scheme for accomplishing His work on earth.

This book spends a lot of time plumbing the depths of Scripture, especially the prophetic literature, to show just how widespread is God's desire to redeem and restore the world. Of particular value is the author's insightful use of Isaiah 65. In Chapter 10, he goes to great lengths to show how practical and relevant is God's intention to bless the world. Thrush's glimpse of a Church intimately involved in bringing about God's new creation is inspiring. It is a refreshing look at how central to the Christian faith are issues that are so often held captive by agenda-driven politicians and a secular media—important, life-giving issues like health care, housing, healthy families, and jobs.

The task of this book, as described by author Lynn Thrush, is to unpack biblical pictures of hope. Indeed, it's a soaring call to imagine life as it ought to be, empty of the fatalism and negativity that is so pervasive in the Church today. It's an invitation to re-imagine the good that the Gospel can accomplish in our lives and the lives of those around us. It's a message of optimism and hope from the heart of God to a world and a Church so desperately in need of good news today.

PERRY L. ENGLE, BISHOP
Pacific and Midwest Conferences
of the Brethren in Christ Church

INTRODUCTION

OVER THE WEEK BETWEEN CHRISTMAS and New Year's Day, my daughter and I were jogging on a beautiful Southern California morning and she wanted to ask a few questions about buying a house. I said, "I believe the willingness to talk about this is more than 50 percent of the journey of buying a house." My wife and I had taken this journey just four years prior. We agreed to explore house-buying, and remarkably that led to actual purchase.

This book calls you to the "more than 50 percent of the journey" of believing the good news of God. Having hope that God's Kingdom will come and His will be done on earth leads to it happening. "According to your faith be it unto you," Jesus said.

I write as a pastor of nearly three and a half decades, and a professor at a Christian university for a fourth of that time. Primarily I help people interpret the Bible. When that task is done faithfully and well, I am persuaded that it points to remarkable hopefulness for life now.

I invite you to imagine life as it ought to be. Spread the good news that God reigns. As you take initiatives based on God's good news, share that with your friends. I would be pleased to hear your story at LynnThrush.com.

Lynn Thrush
Christmas 2011

Part I

WHEN GOOD NEWS GETS ABORTED: WHY THIS BOOK IS IMPORTANT

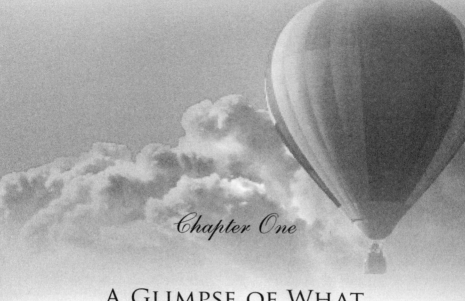

Chapter One

A GLIMPSE OF WHAT COULD BE

FIFTY-FOUR ABORTED BABIES WERE FOUND in a box off a major LA area freeway not far from my home. The year, 1997—a clinic was disposing of these babies, and remarkably, a box tumbled off the truck. Concerned persons organized a memorial service, and I was asked to speak. Individuals were invited to name the babies; our nine-year-old daughter picked the name Zachary David (Zachary means "God has remembered," and David means "Beloved one"). On the day of the service, a procession of fifty-four small white boxes were carried in somber procession to their burial site.

Those fifty-four babies would be about fourteen years old as I write. We will never know, but some of them would be demonstrating musical aptitudes by now. The boys would have men's voices, and the girls would now have their adult bodies. Some of them could be demonstrating language aptitudes, while others could be demonstrating early gifts of wisdom. The tragedy of abortion is that we will never know of these possibilities. The world goes on, there are other things to take up our time, other causes that engage our passions, but we will never know what could have been. It would be nice if somehow we could see those fifty-four stories. It would be nice if we could run the clock back and save those babies, and then run the clock ahead to see all the developments of what might have been.

Thorton Wilder's *Our Town* lets the reader do that. I remember reading that play in eleventh grade, and to this day I remember the impact of that story on me. In the play Emily Gibbs dies in childbirth. After her death she has the opportunity to relive one day of her life, so she chooses her twelfth birthday. While reliving that day, she realizes just how much life should be valued "every, every minute." Poignantly she asks the stage manager whether anyone realizes life while they live it, and she is told, "No. The saints and poets, maybe—they do some."

I want to learn Emily's lesson: I want to value "every, every minute." I believe you do too. In a sense these people in Emily's town were experiencing an abortion of insight. They did not value life, certainly not "every, every minute." For lack of insight, Emily Gibbs did not savor life; she never knew what could have been. If she could have had a glimpse of what could be while she was alive, her story might have been quite different. For her, tragically, her imagination was not released until after she died.

I have observed imaginations squelched, hope aborted. I saw it when my wife miscarried twice after delivering three healthy children. One of the older ladies said to me with resignation reigning in her voice, "I just don't think I could bring children into the world, as bad as the world is." It's a good thing we did not listen to her; the world would have been the poorer for not experiencing the blessing of our fourth child.

I have observed imagination squelched as I study students. It has been my privilege to teach university students for nearly a decade. Many reflect a kind of passivity about faith and life. This is especially so if the sum of faith is "my sins are forgiven and I am going to Heaven"; then the attitude toward the Christian faith slouches: "been there, done that."

In addition to limited imagination aborting hope, I have observed what I am calling *The Sword of Damocles Syndrome*. Damocles thought the king was most fortunate because he was surrounded by magnificence. The king offered to allow Damocles to sit on his throne; but in order to have Damocles understand the pressures of leadership, King Dionysius fastened a huge sword above the throne, held only by the single hair of a horse's tail. Several generations have lived under the constant anticipation of immediate doom. It is self-evident that that experience does not nourish hope; rather, it aborts it.

But what if...what if clichés of doom are not true? What if Jesus answers His prayer that we pray regularly that His Kingdom comes and His will is done on earth as it is in Heaven? What if there really is hope, for now? We could then get glimpses of what could be.

In *The Shawshank Redemption,* that wonderful movie where banker Andy understands a bigger picture than prison, he broadcasts classical music across the loudspeakers of the prison. He spent two weeks in solitary for that stunt, and later told his fellow inmates, "easiest two weeks I have ever done in solitary."

"Why?" they asked. "Did they let you take the music in with you?"

Andy points to his heart and his head. "They can't take music from you."

One of the prisoners tells Andy that hope is a dangerous thing inside a prison. "Hope can drive a man insane."

"In here is where music makes the most sense—so you don't forget that there's something inside they can't touch; it's yours," Andy says.

"What are you talking about?"

"Hope."

The task of this book is to unpack the biblical pictures of hope. The material herein is not new, but the task is necessary because the flame of hope can so easily be minimized or extinguished. Consider today's usage of the word apocalypse, or apocalyptic. It's a transliteration of the Greek word meaning "revealing," a quite wonderful, positive, and magnetic word. The title of the last book of the Bible is the Apocalypse of Jesus Christ. Paul says that creation is waiting with eager longing for the apocalypse/revealing of the children of God (see Rom. 8:19). Waiting for revealing is an activity of eager anticipation. Today, however, apocalypse and apocalyptic are words now meaning something far different. Now the focus is on "sudden, violent end," "one that is unsettling or threatening." Now the word focuses on the "sudden, violent, and destructive." The word has been taken hostage by foreign meanings, and hope has been diminished.

"Things are going to get worse and worse" is a phrase that is underneath a lot of worldviews of persons who call themselves Christians. That's bad news, and Mark opens his gospel with Jesus saying, *"Repent* [from that way of thinking], *and believe the good news that Jesus rules the world."* We'll unpack that text more in the next chapter. How broadly and deeply held is the "worse and worse" perspective? Allow my observations to prompt your own alertness to how persons think about the future.

At the beginning of the semester, I draw on the whiteboard a long line gradually ascending, and a long line gradually descending. Then I ask the mostly freshmen university class, "Which way do you think history is going?" It's a substantially unfair question, and yet it gets at fundamental assumptions about hope, about what one might attempt, about what one might believe to be possible, or perhaps just as importantly, about what will get preached and talked about to the following generation. The question gets about a fifty-fifty response of those willing to give their opinion. Really, the issue is not small is it? It's akin to half the students saying the world is round, and half saying it is flat. It's an assumption with lots of issues related to it.

The question raised in this book is, for how much may we hope in this world? The disciples of Chicken Little will say, "Improvement is not going to happen." (Some will say it with an exclamation point!) Some may believe that ultimately things will improve, but not until Jesus returns and makes everything right. The strength and breadth and length of one's hope influences the sophistication (a more developed, complex, refined form, technique, level) of our response. The story is told of the mountain town with the well-developed ambulance service to care for the many accidents that occurred on a wicked curve in the road. From recruiting drivers to keeping up with the best equipment, this town provided for the victims who did not navigate the turn safely. Then a mother began to hope that accidents would not happen in the first place, and she proposed the idea of cutting a road through the mountain to avoid the curve altogether. This book is about dreaming about cutting roads through mountains, about every valley being raised up, and every mountain and hill made low, about the crooked made straight, and the rough ways made smooth, in the anticipation that all flesh shall see the salvation of God (see Isa. 40:3-5; Luke 3:4-6).

Many students, and congregants alike, think of faith as personal and private. They have less perspective on what God may want from them in the world. When I asked a young lady what was so good about the good news of God, she said she could not wait to go to Heaven to be with Jesus. No doubt that has been what she has been taught. Here was a nineteen-year-old in the bloom of life, and she holds that what is good news about the good news of God is that she gets to go to Heaven to be with Him. She does not have a vision of the good news for this world, and so she emphasizes a personal and private faith that most importantly gets her private self to be privately with God. There's an abortion here. She has no language for hope now. She is not dreaming about what might come to pass now. She and we will never know what might have been accomplished through her for she is not imagining the world as it ought to be. This is tragic tragedy.

Truth be told, this personal, private, and other-worldly version of God's good news is not deeply engaging ensuing generations. The appeal of Heaven and the fear of hell simply are not the heavy hitters they once were. Who knows the reasons? Heaven, for all its other-worldness, is hard to make appealing. It is life in another magnitude and hard to imagine. Then, with the development of housing that comfortably keeps us out of the elements, to all kinds of instant communication, to fabulous medical assistance, to remarkable transportation—well, the contrast between Heaven and earth is not as great as generations ago.

Further, hell is hard to make more scary or awful. Horror movies depict evil and mayhem and cacophony, and news capacity brings us mind-bending and heart-wrenching pain from all around the globe to our televisions and computers and Blackberries. Hell is not as frightening as it once was. The personal, private, bottom-line rationale to enter Heaven and escape hell seems ultimately weak, and getting weaker; and it's not engaging subsequent generations very deeply. It appears people are saying, "I'll take my chances."

To the extent that faith is demonstrated to be for the individual solely, to that extent such persons have the appearance of being marginal, of being out of touch, of being insignificant players in the world. In July 2009 President Barack Obama nominated Evangelical Christian Dr. Francis Collins to head the National Institute of Health. Dr. Collins led the Human Genome Project. He was unanimously confirmed by the Senate. Several news analyses registered surprise that such a one should be named to such an important medical role, and further questioned whether such a person could carry out the duties given his faith stance. Not only, the reports insinuated, are such persons marginal, but indeed their personal, private faith may mitigate against their functioning responsibly in the public square.

There's another rather surprising and disappointing fallout from making faith solely personal and private. Because their Christian faith has little to offer regarding this world, the deduction such persons make is something like this: "Jesus is good for the private stuff; beyond that, if you're smart you'll pack a six-shooter." This kind of faith takes on a variety of characteristics. It can contribute to bad attitudes because the personal-and-private-salvation-only perspective does not understand salvation to have much to do with this current world. Thus when disappointments arise in the world, they contribute to these persons becoming irritable and angry. Everything is at risk in this view. There is no calm assurance about the world in this faith that is solely about Jesus and me.

Private faith can lead not only to bad attitudes, but this understanding of faith contributes to these persons taking up the wisdom and weapons of the flesh. The weapons of their warfare are worldly: F16s, bazookas, land mines, hand guns, and war. So while Jesus is in Heaven, while we wait for Him to take over, we'll fight with the best six-shooter technology we have. And when Jesus comes back, He'll iron-fist His enemies like we do now, only His iron fist is more effective than ours. Nya, nya, nya.

By the way, fear sells. You can gather crowds to hear a diet of fear. It's kind of odd, when you think about it, being drawn to fear, but it works. "You better know what *they* are up to, or you will be overcome." "If we don't wake up, the Church will be destroyed." "They are going to overtake the world." "They are about world domination." "Come hear the secret story of how they are infiltrating us." "Come hear how you can defend your faith against them." "If such and such happens, you can be sure we will not last much longer." "How to protect your wealth." "What to do before everything collapses." It's kind of hard to be joy-filled after a diet of this, isn't it? It's difficult to be hopeful. And frankly, I do not see world-changers among my friends who live on this steady diet of fear. Their imagination for good has been aborted, and the world does not experience what might arise out of their healthy imagination. It is abortion when imagination is ripped from one's life by the scissors of fear. Tragedy, indeed.

Now the person I am describing can indeed believe that things are going to get better, that the beautiful pictures of God's rule working in the world is indeed ahead; oh, but there's a catch. The catch effectively denudes one of the necessity of praying for, expecting, and working for the Kingdom on earth. "When will this happen?" I regularly get asked this question when speaking on this subject. A common assumption is, "This will happen after the second coming of Jesus." End of discussion. End of hope for this world. End of imagining what might happen. Why? Because the assumption is deeply held, "Those good things occur after Jesus returns the second time." Another abortion. We'll never know what this one might have imagined for this world, might have prayed for, might have hoped for, might have worked for. Tragic.

I'll not forget the startling possibility I encountered as I was reading from New Testament scholar, biblical theologian, and accomplished author N.T. Wright. He wrote that first century Jews did not expect the end of the world as we know it. I was stunned. I have always expected the end of the world. But what if God does not plan to destroy this earth, but restore it? What are the implications? We'll get to some of the biblical references that may be coming to your mind right now, but if it is the case that the assumption that God has in mind to incinerate His earth and make a new one is not correct, then there are a sea-change of considerations before us. Maybe it is not so unwise to cut a road through the mountain.

This writer grew up with influential authors and preachers assuring us that history would conclude within a generation of 1948. I have in my files a booklet, "88 reasons Jesus will return again in 1988." Theological schools, publishing houses, television and radio broadcasts, magazines, and devotional guides grew up around that guiding light that history could close at any moment, and most probably would be closing in some relation to 1948.

How keenly I felt this as a youngster. I remember in junior high school I was in a Chess Club tournament, I in the winner's bracket, my friend, in the loser's bracket. I needed but one more victory to be the champion. In the class immediately before Chess Club, I had a Social Studies class, and we had a test that day. At the end of the test the teacher said that three persons had cheated, and should let her know on the way out. I had cheated, and I spoke to the teacher about that. Though I had confessed to the teacher, I was deeply concerned that the Lord might have returned during the time right after I had cheated and before I had confessed. During Chess Club I desperately wanted to see my cousin walk past the door of my room. If I saw my cousin through the door, I would know that the Lord had not returned. Alas, she did not pass the door, and alas, thoroughly distracted, I lost not one but two games. For many years the Queen's trophy (rather than the King's) sat on my bedroom mantle as a witness not to cheat, and as a witness to my anticipation of the near close of history.

"The soon return of the Lord" was a phrase oft used, and those of us influenced by that teaching got the point loud and clear: we were the last generation. You could do the math: we may have time to get married, hopefully so, but we did not envision ourselves as grandparents. That would be two generations after 1948. No, we were assured the Lord was returning soon. Occasionally a specific day has been chosen. Harold Camping claimed the world was coming to an end on May 21, 2011. Shortly before that day I saw him being interviewed on a Los Angeles television station; I saw pictures of billboards on Internet news, and read some of the stories of young couples who had emptied their savings in anticipation of the end of the world. For certain these young people were not planning how to make the world better; they were getting ready to leave.

I have in my office a picture frame with a statement: "Nothing happens without conversation. When that kicks in, anything can happen." Rodney Stark, in his book *To the Glory of God,* does a wonderful extended chapter/mini-book on the rise of science within Christianity, and he says Christianity was necessary for the rise of science because Christianity's view of God as faithful, dependable, consistent, and orderly opened the way for Christians to imagine that God's creation could be explored because it likely shared these traits of its Creator. Stark observes that science was not attempted in other cultures/religions. His deduction: "No one will attempt what philosophically they believe to be impossible."[1]

That is precisely the point of this book. I maintain there has been an abortion of hope. Our imaginations have been squelched, because we have been told that things are going to get worse and worse, and that's an untold tragedy. I will be making the case from the Scripture that there is soaring hope, and I will invite us to imagine the world as it ought to be. One coed, after studying the Scripture about God's good news for this world wrote, "I am deeply hopeful." When this is the testimony of an eighteen-year-old, the foundation is in place for the Spirit to work mightily in her imagination. To participate in the unleashing of the imagination that springs from irrepressible hope for our world, this is an endeavor to which I am delighted to give myself, and to which I invite you to join. We look next at the biblical expectations that contradict hopelessness for this world. If we will allow, we may find that the good news of God is far better news than we first imagined. Oh to get a glimpse of what could be!

ENDNOTE

1. Rodney Stark, *For the Glory of God* (Princeton, NJ: Princeton University Press, 2003), 151.

Part II

Biblical Expectations that Contradict Hopelessness

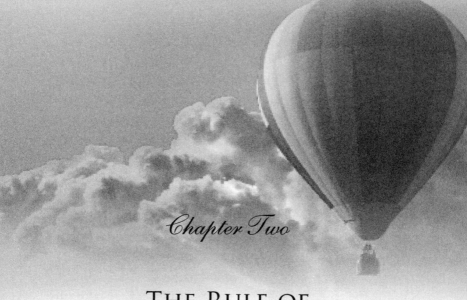

Chapter Two

THE RULE OF
GOD—NOW

I CAN REMEMBER WHEN HIV/AIDS was discovered. I remember how substantially it was connected to homosexuality. At the time there was no known cure, and it seemed like it was the judgment of God duly being administered to those who did not follow His ways. In fact I remember the thought that to try to find a cure for AIDS could be conceived as disrespecting God's judgment.

The spring 2011 edition of the Brethren in Christ magazine, *In Part,* has this cover story, "The End of AIDS?" This story about AIDS started because of the dramatic success with malaria treatment headed by Dr. Phil Thuma, and in partnership with Johns Hopkins University School of Public Health in Baltimore. In the ten years from 2001-2011, malaria cases at Macha in Zambia were reduced by 95 percent. Because of this tremendous success with malaria,

Dr. Thuma and Dr. John Spurrier began to set their sights on HIV/AIDS. Anti-Retroviral Therapy was showing great promise. Said Dr. Spurrier, "We've started down this path, and we're beginning to dream and ask ourselves the question, 'Could the Brethren in Christ mission in Macha be one of the first places in the world to eliminate AIDS?'"[1]

The work of these two doctors contradicts the message that there is no hope for this world. In Part II of this book we review several themes from the Bible that contradict hopelessness. The first of these themes is the rule of God—now. A middle-aged man in my congregation, when he heard the topic on which I was writing said, "Make sure you include the part about the Kingdom of God present in Christ." He was drawn to this good news, and I believe you will be drawn as well.

"Now… Jesus came to Galilee proclaiming the good news of God" (Mark 1:14). I would have liked to have heard Him talking about the good news of God, wouldn't you? It's an interesting phrase: the good news of God. If it's good news for God, it must really be good news. And Jesus would be an authority on the good news, wouldn't He? I wonder how Jesus described this good news? But then, wonderfully, Mark records the summary of Jesus' explanation. Here it is: "the time has come." Time is the Greek word *kairos*, not *chronos*, from which we get the word chronology. *Kairos* is the word for time that denotes great significance. The *kairos* has come. The Kingdom of God—the rule of God *"aggiken,"* has come. Our English texts say, "Has come near," or "is at hand." Dallas Willard explains that it means "has come," or "is here."[2]

The problem with the phrases "is near," and "at hand," is that we English speakers emphasize precisely the opposite of "here." If I were to say, "The ship is near the Long Beach dock," you would think, "the ship is near, but the ship is not here." If I say, "The meal is at hand," you will likely understand that the meal is very close to being served, but it is, nevertheless, not at the point of being served. So we come away from Jesus' message denuding it of its intended impact. "The rule of God is here" is the meaning that makes sense. Jesus would not use the word *kairos,* nor would He say the *kairos* is fulfilled, if He is merely meaning that He is talking about something that is indefinitely removed from what He was saying, perhaps even by 2,000 years or more. No, His first phrase, *"the time is fulfilled,"* and His second phrase, *"the kingdom of God is here"* are two ways of saying the same thing. The good news of God is that in Jesus the rule of God has come into the world. Everyone is to drop any other view of history, and believe in the good news that the rule of God has come (see Mark 1:15).

Some years ago the church in North America lived through the avant-garde theological movement of spiritual mapping and spiritual warfare. Benefits were substantial to a church that needed to grow in the alertness to the spirit world. However, the diminishing of Jesus as the Ruler, of His rule having come in Himself, was harmful in that Satan was elevated as the effective ruler of the world, and he and his ways needed to be understood. Spiritual warfare tended to be taken from its biblical context, as described above, and it became significantly Gnostic, with secret knowledge and secret insight at a premium. But the news that gives a preponderance of time to the bad news is not as good as the good news of God. And fundamentally we are called to believe the truth that the good news of God has come in Jesus Christ.

Often Satan is given so much credit that persons believe that he is the ruler of this world now. I'm not sure if the rule of Satan is easier to understand, easier to illustrate, easier to accept, or perhaps all three are true. I remember a lady coming to me one time in significant fear. She had received one of those chain letters that threatened that if you stopped it something bad would happen to you. She believed it. She did not want to keep the chain letter going, but she was afraid to stop it. So I invited her to give the letter to me, and with substantial relief, she did.

It is a biblically fair question to ask, when considering the present rule of God, where is Satan currently? John records Jesus' teaching in John 12:31, *"Now is the judgment of this world; now the ruler of this world will be driven out."* The author in Hebrews 2:14 writes, *"Since, therefore, the children share flesh and blood, he* [Jesus] *himself likewise shared the same things, so that through death he might destroy the one who has the power of death, that is, the devil."* John adds more emphasis in his first letter, First John 3:8, *"The Son of God was revealed for this purpose, to destroy the works of the devil."* And, if one will allow, Revelation 20 may refer to this subject also. John could be saying what he said in John 12:31. Clearly the devil is being bound. Given that Jesus is the One who casts out the ruler of this world, who destroys the devil, who destroys the works of the devil, it makes sense that He is the One who binds Satan and throws him into the bottomless pit.

One might be thinking about how this teaching fits with Peter's words that the devil prowls around like a roaring lion, looking for someone to devour (see 1 Pet. 5:8). That text needs to fit with the other texts of Scripture about the devil. It's interesting what prophylactics are prescribed against the devil: humility, do not hold on to anxieties, practice discipline, keep alert, resist him, stand firm in your faith, and importantly, know that your brothers and sisters throughout the world are undergoing the same kinds of sufferings.

Suffering has common components the world over. One component is that we are called to be humble (see 1 Pet. 5:5-6). It is a suffering experience to live humbly, but in due time God exalts us. He exalts us, restores us, supports us, strengthens us, and establishes us (see 1 Pet. 5:10). We are also called to cast all our anxiety on Him, because He cares for us (see 1 Pet. 5:7). It is a suffering experience to live with anxiety, but in due time He will restore, support, strengthen, and establish us (see 1 Pet. 5:10). Peter describes the suffering of living with discipline and being vigilant. It is a suffering experience to live with discipline, to be vigilant about sexual integrity, financial integrity, and handling power with integrity, but God Himself restores, supports, strengthens, and establishes us (see 1 Pet. 5:10). To Him be the power forever. Amen (see 1 Pet. 5:11). When we are proud, we get eaten up by the devil. When we are anxious, we get eaten up by the devil. When we are undisciplined and not vigilant, we get eaten up by the devil (see 1 Pet. 5:8). I read that, like all cats, lions have very good acceleration, but little stamina. Biblical authors are confident that resisting the devil results in the devil fleeing (see James 4:7; 1 Pet. 5:9).

Peter's teaching supports what John, Paul, and Jesus teach about the devil. He is no ruling ruler. Jesus has deposed him; he functions more like a scavenger. If he sees someone who is not alert, like a lamb that has gotten separated from the flock, that one is a candidate to be eaten up. Thus we see the devil is not a ruler, a powerful boss. The devil does not have authority like a ruler does. The devil does not have power as does the ruler. The devil does not have the role of overseeing a well-ordered society. The Scriptures teach his incapacitation, particularly through the death and resurrection of Jesus.

All of this sounds very close to the teaching of Paul in Second Corinthians 2:11, *"we are not ignorant of his* [Satan's] *designs."* There the issue is forgiveness. Paul looks to have a good attitude precisely so that he is not outwitted by Satan.

So it is that when we are about to speak on the rule of God and the Kingdom of God we can appropriately embrace the strong words of Scripture that Satan has been defanged and defeated by Jesus Christ through His death and resurrection. We need not, indeed ought not, imagine that Satan is an equal rival ruler; he is not. But Peter, James, and Paul teach that if one fails to be diligent in attitude then one can be devoured, essentially by default. Living humbly, casting our anxieties on Christ, living with discipline and vigilance—in so living we resist the devil, and encouragingly he flees and God draws near.

Let's return to the implications of believing the good news of God, that in Jesus Christ the rule of God has come. I referred to Rodney Stark's wonderful statement, "Fundamental theological and philosophical assumptions determine whether anyone will attempt to do science." As Stark looked at other cultures, he deduced as follows: "It did not occur to the Chinese that science was possible." One could fairly say, "It does not occur to many people that the rule of God is present, and thus that Kingdom behavior in this world is required and Kingdom results are to be anticipated." The declaration of the rule of God in this world is the passion that drives this book.

Mark's opening announcement, Mark 1:14-15, is pregnant with significance. Jesus uses the word *kairos*. He is talking about significant time; He's talking about an historic moment. He's talking about God's action in history. This is an unrepeatable moment—kairos. Then, *"peplarotai"*—is fulfilled, filled up, completed. This significant time is filled full with its potential meaning.

My wife and I have had the privilege of many people sitting around our holiday table for a turkey dinner: turkey, filling, gravy, mashed potatoes, Swiss vegetable medley (with Swiss cheese), sweet potatoes (with marshmallow topping), pink salad, crescent rolls, butter, jelly, pickles, olives, cranberry salad, French apple pie, vanilla ice cream, water, iced tea, coffee—fulfilled. The expectations of the holiday meal are fully completed. Jesus said the *kairos*, this significant moment is filled full with meaning and substance.

The *basileia* of God—the Kingdom of God—the rule of God—the kingship of God begins the second parallel description in Mark 1:15. David and Karen Mains wrote two marvelous children/adult books: *Tales of the Kingdom* and *Tales of the Resistance.* The protagonist was learning to "sight" the king. "Sightings" involved some certain abilities to "see" the king. Jesus was going around speaking of this Kingdom of God, this concept of the arena where the rule of God is practiced, is followed, where the kingship of God is acknowledged. We are invited to "see" this rule, and to participate in this rule.

This Kingdom of God *"aggiken,"* is here; this word is the perfect tense of *eggizo,* to bring near, to approach, to come near, to be at hand. The perfect tense "implies a process, but views that process as having reached its consummation and existing in a finished state."[3] This is remarkably, incredibly, wonderfully good news! History can now go in the right direction. This is the good news about which this book is written.

This is a "fundamental theological and philosophical assumption" is it not? And this assumption will determine what and how much we attempt. If it does not occur to us that the rule of God is possible, or that the rule of God is effective now, then we simply will not be thinking and praying and working toward that end, nor will we be thinking about implications of such. South Africa's Bishop Desmond Tutu believed that the good news of God, the rule of God, meant that apartheid ought not continue. The ultimate law of the universe is not "que sera, sera, whatever will be, will be." South Africa changed. Justice prevailed, and this book ends with a testimony out of that setting of one of the most hopeful stories imaginable.

Jesus went around speaking about what was good news to God; indeed it was good news from God. What God had been looking for all through history had now arrived. It had not only arrived, but all the benchmarks of its significance were present and filled full with meaning and promise. Thus Jesus explained: God's rule has arrived; it has come. Where God's rule is in effect, creation works as it ought. Incredible, competent love is at the center of the universe. This is indeed good news!

The next word is "repent." Why do you imagine Jesus uses this word? From what is one repenting? Would it be fair to say one is to repent from believing bad news? And would bad news be that the rule of Satan is in place? Repent from that. Change your mind about that. Believe the good news.

Once our Church Board was discussing ways in which we could grow, and one board member said, after hearing the discussion about more persons being part of our congregation, "I'll believe it when I see it." Fascinatingly, Jesus invites us to believe the good news of God's rule before we see it. He did not say, "Watch and wait. You will see that God's rule has come, and when you see it you should then believe." No, He calls us to believe His good news, "sight unseen," using a phrase with which I grew up. Indeed this book is about overcoming the tragedy of the squelched imagination, and what we believe is critical to the function of the imagination. When we believe in the present rule of God that has come in the Lord Christ, we appropriately ask, indeed want to ask, "What are the implications of believing this good news?" Certainly the present rule of Christ contradicts the mantra, "Of course things are going to get worse and worse."

There is no need to downplay the reality of God's rule. Of course all is not yet as it ought to be, but that does not take away from Jesus saying that God's Kingdom had come, or that we should not pray for His Kingdom to come and will to be done on earth as it is in Heaven. Of course the land of Canaan had obstacles for Israel, but the land was flowing with milk and honey, and they were to take the land that God was giving them. What Israel needed to focus on then, and what we need to focus on now, is God's ability, His promise. We are called to believe the promise. That's where the emphasis needs to be made.

Ralph Winter, a missiologist, was a great one to think about the implications of the Kingdom being present. He proposed that cancer research is Kingdom work; it overcomes the destroying work of cancer. He proposed patterns for education as a means of cooperating with God's work in the world. His vision for God's people possessing the land was broad and expansive.

At the beginning of this chapter I told the story of two Brethren in Christ doctors in Zambia, Africa. Dr. Phil Thuma worked in partnership with Johns Hopkins University School of Public Health to dramatically reduce the number of malaria cases in that area.

Because of that success he and Dr. John Spurrier began to set their sights on eradicating the HIV/AIDS virus. In March 2005 Macha Hospital opened its Anti-Retroviral Therapy clinic, which offered the treatment at no charge. One afternoon in 2009 when Dr. Spurrier was about to head home, a man walked in with his wife, toddler-aged twins, and a nursing infant. Dr. Spurrier looked at the family's patient files. In 2007 the man came in with HIV/AIDS; he had lost twenty to twenty-five pounds, was very ill, and could no longer care for his family at home. A month later his wife came with the twins, and the whole family was started on Anti-Retroviral Therapy.

As Dr. Spurrier now looked at the patient file for the baby he was astounded to see that the baby was HIV-negative. "Normally" the family would be very sick and some would have died, but now they were living in the truly normal way, the father planting his fields, the mother cooking and caring for the family, the twins active, and the baby HIV-negative.

Because hopelessness has been contradicted, these doctors are moving ahead to treat what had seemed untreatable. Possibilities in one area began to open up possibilities in another. Comprehending the rule of God provides foundation for working to bring about His purposes on earth. Believing this rule of God is the fuel that drives the engine of action. Based on the rule of God, we move to possess the land. This great enterprise to possess the land also contradicts hopelessness. To this we now turn.

ENDNOTES

1. Kristine N. Frey, "The End of AIDS?" *In Part: The Magazine for the Brethren in Christ Community in North America,* Spring 2011, 6.

2. Dallas Willard, *The Divine Conspiracy* (San Francisco, CA: HarperSanFrancisco, 1997), 28.

3. H.E. Dana and Julius R. Mantey, *A Manual of the Greek New Testament* (New York: Macmillan Publishing Company, Inc., 1955), 200.

Chapter Three

POSSESS THE LAND—THE SOIL OF DREAMS

THE FARM ON WHICH I grew up was the same farm on which my father had lived for sixty-five years, since he was ten years of age. We did not possess the land in terms of owning it, and after those many years the farm was sold. Today not a trace remains of the farm; it is developed with townhouses, apartments, and single-family dwellings. Because my family did not possess that land, the land ended up serving the purposes of another.

In the movie, *Music of the Heart,* a white, middle-class school teacher is plunged into the heart of a problem-ridden inner city Harlem school. Meryl Streep plays the violin teacher, Roberta Guaspari, and the teacher possesses the land. How? Through discipline and sheer force of her own determination children learn to play and perform well, and skeptical parents become supportive. Then, after ten years, the school board shuts her classes down. Guaspari stages, along with help from a number of the world's premiere violinists, an amazing fundraising concert at Carnegie Hall, the proceeds from which save the program. This violin teacher possessed the land.

The language of possessing the land is a rich and important theme in Scripture. When Abraham demonstrated his willingness to sacrifice Isaac in obedience to God's instruction, Abraham's willingness to offer his only son elicited remarkable promises from God. God would bless Abraham. God would make his offspring as numerous as the stars and the sand (see Gen. 22:17). All nations would be blessed by way of Abraham's offspring, and particularly, for the purposes of our thinking here, Abraham's offspring would possess the gate of their enemies. (Some translations say, *"take possession of the cities of their enemies."*)

Abraham heard those promises clearly. We would have heard those promises too. When someone speaks an affirming word to us, painting a positive prophetic picture of a good future, we remember such. Indeed we often share that with our network. Abraham told his family about this scintillating future. We know that because when Abraham sent his servant to Abraham's own country to get a wife for his son Isaac, we hear this very promise spoken. When Rebekah's family sent her with Abraham's servant, they blessed her by saying, *"May you, our sister, become thousands of myriads; may your offspring gain possession of the gates of their foes"* (Gen. 24:60). They had heard about the remarkable promise to Uncle Abraham, that his descendants would possess the cities of their enemies. Now, to have their daughter/sister marry into Abraham's line! Wow! And so they repeated that prophetic picture to Rebekah in the form of a blessing, *"May your offspring possess the gates of their enemies."*

Of course this promise becomes especially significant to all of us who are descendants of Abraham. Paul makes it clear in Romans 4 that Abraham is the ancestor of all who believe, those circumcised and those not circumcised (see Rom. 4:11-12,16). We stand in line to have these words spoken to us, *"May your offspring possess the gates of their enemies."* At my son and daughter-in-law's wedding I used the Genesis 24:60 text. It's for them, and for us. In the course of this chapter we shall want to explore the concept of possession. It includes themes of ownership, responsibility, privilege, investment, and hopefulness. How pregnant are these terms! You, I, we are to possess the land.

Because the biblical theme possession of the land seems to me to be not widely understood, I want to illustrate its importance by noting many, not all, passages that include the theme. Understanding the theme of possessing the land becomes compost, the soil of dreams. It's a remarkably energizing call/theme. Possibilities emerge when you read these biblical texts with an understanding of what possessing the land involves: to have and hold as property, own, to take into one's possession, to enter into and control firmly, to dominate, to bring or cause to fall under influence, possession, or control. Possess can expand to mean: develop, explore, create, master, invest in, make fruitful, multiply assets, enrich, reflect upon, dream, make better, take responsibility for, care for, assist, make something to be as good as it can be, take initiative, be steward of—what a wonderfully pregnant concept!

Ted Byfield is the editor of the very excellent twelve volume series *The Christians: Their First Two Thousand Years*. He has been a journalist for sixty-five years. I learned about his name in that he was the visionary behind *The Christian History Project*; he served as general editor of the first six volumes of this series. That project became insolvent; and so in 2005 he formed SEARCH, The Society to Explore and Record Christian History. That endeavor has continued to publish volumes seven through ten as I write this chapter. Byfield is the president of SEARCH, and continues as general editor of the series, *The Christians: Their First Two Thousand Years*. Ted Byfield has possessed the land.

We would do well to reflect a bit here at the outset of thinking about possessing the land. There's a vast difference between 1) *"not lacking anything,"* (see Deut. 2:7), while not possessing the land, essentially wondering throughout the vast desert of life, and 2) possessing the land. The generation of the children of Israel that came up out of Egypt did not possess the land. God supplied their needs, but what a dramatically different agenda is merely having our needs met, rather than possessing the land!

Indeed the call to possess the land was paramount for God's people: *"See, I have set the land before you; go in and take possession of the land that I swore to your ancestors, to Abraham, to Isaac, and to Jacob, to give to them and to their descendants after them"* (Deut. 1:8).

In Deuteronomy 28 Moses makes possession of the land an issue of obedience. Either we are possessing the land, or we are being scattered and destroyed. There is not really a middle ground. Notice the cost of disobedience in not possessing the land:

> The Lord will make the pestilence cling to you until it has consumed you off the land that you are entering to possess (see Deut. 28:21). You shall build a house, but not live in it. You shall plant a vineyard, but not enjoy its fruit (see Deut. 28:30). (This is precisely opposite of the new creation picture of Isaiah 65:21-22.) Just as the Lord took delight in making you prosperous and numerous, so the Lord will take delight in bringing you to ruin and destruction; you shall be plucked off the land that you are entering to possess (see Deut. 28:63).

Joshua's commission was precisely possession of the land:

> *Be strong and courageous; for you shall put this people in possession of the land that I swore to their ancestors to give them* (Joshua 1:6).

Possession involved work:

> *The hill country shall be yours, for though it is a forest, you shall clear it and possess it to its farthest borders; for you shall drive out the Canaanites, though they have chariots of iron, and though they are strong* (Joshua 17:18).

Possession involves taking initiative:

So Joshua said to the Israelites, "How long will you be slack about going in and taking possession of the land that the Lord, the God of your ancestors has given you? (Joshua 18:3)

Possession involves surveying, understanding the terrain, and then dividing it up in manageable sizes, and assigning responsibility for possession (see Josh. 18:4-6, 8-10). Sometimes possession is hard (see Josh. 19:47), as when the territory of the Danites was lost to them, and they had to fight to recapture it, take possession, and settle in it. Near the end of Joshua's book this summary is given:

Thus the Lord gave to Israel all the land that he swore to their ancestors that he would give them; and having taken possession of it, they settled there. And the Lord gave them rest on every side just as he had sworn to their ancestors; not one of all their enemies had withstood them, for the Lord had given all their enemies into their hands. Not one of all the good promises that the Lord had made to the house of Israel had failed; all came to pass (Joshua 21:43-45).

Indeed, the good promises of God have to do with the agenda of possession. In Joshua 24:2-4,8,13, Joshua said to all the people:

Thus says the Lord, the God of Israel: Long ago your ancestors—Terah and his sons Abraham and Nahor—lived beyond the Euphrates and served other gods. Then I took your father Abraham from beyond the river and led him through all the land of Canaan and made his offspring many. I gave him Isaac; and to Isaac I gave Jacob and Esau. I gave Esau the hill country of Seir to possess, but Jacob and his children went down to Egypt. Then I brought you to the land of the Amorites, who lived on the other side of the Jordan; they fought with you and I handed them over to you, and you took possession of their land, and I destroyed them before you. I gave you a land on which you had not labored, and towns that you had not built, and you live in them; you eat the fruit of vineyards and olive groves that you did not plant.

When the history of Israel under the judges is written the charge to possess the land is compromised.

*The Lord was with Judah, and he took possession of the hill country, **but** could not drive out the inhabitants of the plain* (Judges 1:19).

The Benjamites did not drive out the Jebusites... (Judges 1:21).

Manasseh did not drive out the inhabitants of... or Taanoah...or Dor...or Iblean...or Megiddo.... When Israel grew strong, they put the Canaanites to forced labor, but did not in fact drive them out. And Ephraim did not drive out the Canaanites who lived in Gezer. Zebulun did not drive out the inhabitants of Kitron or Nahalol.... Asher did not drive out the inhabitants of Acco or Sidon or Ahlab or Achzib or Helbah or Aphik or Rehob (Judges 1:27-31).

Naphtali did not drive out the inhabitants of Beth-shemesh or Beth-anath... (Judges 1:33).

Compromising with ungodliness leads to God not clearing away those things that stand in the way of land that is to be possessed. God: *"I will never break my covenant with you. ...But you have not obeyed my command. See what you have done! So now I say, I will not drive them out before you; but they shall become adversaries to you"* (see Judg. 2:1-3). It is appropriate to weep when we are not participating in possession. *"When the angel of the Lord spoke these words to the Israelites, the people lifted up their voices and wept"* (see Judg. 2:4).

At Joshua's death the sad commentary follows, *"that whole generation was gathered to their ancestors, and another generation grew up after them, who did not know the Lord or the work that he had done for Israel"* (Judg. 2:10). Knowing the Lord, and what He did for Israel, has to do with understanding His promise and desire for His people to possess the land/earth. Rather than possessing, Israel was possessed, *"So the anger of the Lord was kindled against Israel, and he gave them over to plunderers who plundered them, and sold them into the power of their enemies all around, so that they could no longer withstand their enemies"* (Judg. 2:14).

Near the end of writing this book, I received the startling news that I had an aggressive prostate cancer. One of my assignments was to read a large book by Patrick Walsh, *Surviving Prostate Cancer.* I learned about cancer cells. If the body "possesses the land," if it carries on with orderly cells, well and good; but if the body is not functioning this way, then the cancer cells begin possessing the good cells. So possessing the land is not optional. It's not for only who we might think to be the super-spiritual. Possessing the land is every person's call. It's the Church's call.

From Israel's earliest calling, they were promised that they would possess the gates of their enemies. It was a promise, a promise concurrent with God's promise that through Abraham all nations would be blessed. Israel had some success, but then they began to relax, and when they did not carefully follow the agenda to possess the land, Israel was in trouble. In relatively short order Israel would be sent into exile.

Being sent out of the land Israel was to possess is clearly failure. Exile is the polar opposite to possessing the land. The prophets served Israel in the context of the Exile. Some speak in anticipation of Exile, as did Isaiah. Some speak while Israel is in Exile, as did Ezekiel, while some reflected upon the Exile after Judah returned from Exile, as did Zechariah. Importantly, possessing the land takes on wider significance than only returning to the geography from which Israel was expelled. Now, to anticipate this book's argument, possessing the land will mean possessing the whole earth, it will mean possessing vocations (jobs) of all sorts.

Because possessing the land is such a deeply important biblical theme, and because the prophets expand that concept in anticipation of Jesus' world-encompassing gospel, I want to illustrate from three prophets and their three vantage points relative to the Exile: Isaiah—before, Ezekiel—during, and Zechariah—afterward.

Isaiah's Message about Possessing the Land

At the outset of his writing Isaiah anticipates the magnetic attraction of God's truth to the nations. Many peoples will say to one another, *"Come, let us go up to the mountain of the Lord,to the house of the God of Jacob;that he may teach us his waysand that we may walk in his paths"* (Isa. 2:3).

Hints of possession are seen in Isaiah 6:3 as seraphs call, *"Holy, holy, holy is the Lord Almighty; the whole earth is full of his glory."* In the remarkable picture of Kingdom life in Jesus in Isaiah 11, the Lord will reclaim the remnant from many places in the world, indeed from the four quarters of the earth (see verse 12). God's people, Ephraim and Judah, will "lay hands" on their enemies, and the enemies "will be subject to them," (see verse 14), that is, God's people will possess them.

Isaiah describes a remarkable way of possessing the land in Isaiah 14:2, *"The nations will take [the people of God] to their place,"* but remarkably, note, *"the house of Israel* [God's people] *will possess the nations as slaves in the Lord's land; they will take captive those who were their captors, and rule over those who oppressed them."* Thus Isaiah describes a possessing by His people, even though His people should be taken captive (see Isa. 14:1-3). That picture of possession broadens in Isaiah 57:13, *"Whoever takes refuge in me shall possess the land and inherit my holy mountain."*

In Isaiah 19:19 he anticipates a remarkable possession in Egypt and Assyria, in addition to Israel; in that day (the day of Jesus) there will be an altar to the Lord in the heart of Egypt, and a monument to the Lord at its border.

Beautifully Isaiah sees a picture of the whole earth filled with God's glory: on that day Israel will be the third with Egypt and Assyria, a blessing in the midst of the earth, *"Blessed be Egypt my people, and Assyria the work of my hands, and Israel my heritage"* (Isa. 19:25). This picture of God working powerfully in and through former enemies of God's people, Egypt and Assyria, is thrilling! Well I remember an Egyptian follower of Jesus in our home, and I asked if Isaiah 19 was a favorite text of her people, and her eyes filled with tears as she said, "Yes." Oh to have our imaginations filled with this expectation!

Isaiah has a tranquil pastoral picture of possessing the land in Isaiah 32:12-20. Here the concept of land is expanded beyond geography to encompass the Spirit's work. *"till the Spirit is poured on us from on high, and the desert becomes a fertile field, and the fertile field seems like a forest. The Lord's justice will dwell in the desert, his righteousness live in the fertile field. The fruit of that righteousness will be peace; its effect will be quietness and confidence forever. My people will live in peaceful dwelling places, in secure homes, in undisturbed places of rest"* (Isa. 32:15-18 NIV). Further, God's people will sow their seed by every stream, and let their cattle and donkeys range freely. What a beautiful image of possessing the land!

The theme of possession of the land grows rich and substantive. In Isaiah 49:8-9 (NIV) the Lord says, *"In the time of my favor I will answer you, and in the day of salvation I will help you; I will keep you and will make you to be a covenant for the people, to restore the land and to reassign its desolate inheritances, to say to the captives,*

'Come out,' and to those in darkness, *'Be free!'* Also see Isaiah 49:13,20,22; these are texts that picture the action of possessing the land.

Isaiah continues to anticipate this bright future for God's people, even though Exile was coming. God's instruction in Isaiah 54:2-3 is thrilling: enlarge the place of your tent, stretch your curtain wide, do not hold back; lengthen your cords, strengthen your stakes. For you will spread out to the right and to the left; your descendents will possess the nations and settle the desolate towns. Here Isaiah reiterates the promise given to Abraham in Genesis 22:17.

Isaiah 57:13 expands the concept of possession further, *"Whoever takes refuge in me shall possess the land and inherit my holy mountain."* How close this is to Jesus' words in Matthew 5:5, *"Blessed are the meek, for they will inherit the earth* [land]. *"* Isaiah says further in 66:2, *"This is the one to whom I will look, to the humble and contrite in spirit, who trembles at my word."*

In the marvelous song of Isaiah 60-66 the prophet begins:

> *Arise, shine; for your light has come, and the glory of the Lord has risen upon you. For darkness shall cover the earth, and thick darkness the peoples; but the Lord will arise upon you, and his glory will appear over you. Nations shall come to your light, and kings to the brightness of your dawn* (Isaiah 60:1-3).

Later in this rich chapter Isaiah repeats, *"Your people* [God's people] *shall all be righteous; they shall possess the land forever"* (verse 21). This thrilling news continues in

Isaiah 61. God's people will be called a planting of the Lord (verse 3). They will rebuild the ancient ruins and restore the places long devastated; they will renew the ruined cities that have been devastated for generations (verse 4). Thus God's people shall possess a double portion. Everlasting joy shall be theirs (verse 7). Hallelujah! "[The descendants of God's people] *shall be known among the nations, and their offspring among the peoples; all who see them shall acknowledge that they are a people whom the Lord has blessed"* (Isa. 61:9). These texts are possession texts.

Are you tracking with this glorious good news? All of Isaiah 62 describes the possession of the land theme. The vindication of the people of God shall be clear as a crown of beauty in the hand of God (verses 1-3). God's people are to be renowned throughout the earth (verse 7). No longer will God's people be called Desolate. Rather, God's people and their land will be called *"My Delight Is in Her,"* and *"Married,"* respectively (verse 4).

Then there is the action of possessing: *"Pass through, pass through the gates! Prepare the way for the people. Build up, build up the highway! Remove the stones. Raise a banner for the nations"* (Isa. 62:10 NIV). Passing through the gates, building up the highway, clearing it of stones, putting up a banner: these are the components of possession.

In Isaiah 65:9 (NIV), God declares, *"I will bring forth descendents from Jacob, and from Judah those who will possess My mountains; My chosen people will inherit them, and there will My servants live."*

And Isaiah 65:17-25 is perhaps the most comprehensive, beautiful, and hopeful picture of God's people possessing the land. All will live long lives. Disease will be increasingly eliminated. Home ownership, jobs, entrepreneurship, and jobs that are rewarding will be reality. Family life will be satisfying. Spiritual vitality and intimacy with God will be experienced. Reconciliation will everywhere be practiced, and there will be neither harm nor destruction practiced.

The possession of the land theme in Isaiah is whole-earth, *"Heaven is my throne and the earth is my footstool"* (Isa. 66:1). Here the land is not local, nor is God's presence confined to a local spot. Mission and evangelism is whole-earth, *"They shall bring your kindred from all nations as an offering to the Lord"* (Isa. 66:20). Persons from all nations will become part of God's Kingdom, God's people.

Some 150 years prior to the Exile, Isaiah was reflecting on the day when God's people would possess the land. It was a comprehensive possession. How powerfully positive was this word, given that Judah was headed in the direction of Exile. How hopeful it must have been to those who heard the message of Isaiah! Today Isaiah's text has a similar impact on us. We do not see possession of the land in full fruition, but Isaiah's scintillating prophecy places markers before us to which we reach. What encouragement! Like Isaiah we can anticipate possession of the land prior to its full implementation. But oh, how important the anticipation is!

EZEKIEL'S MESSAGE ABOUT POSSESSING THE LAND

Ezekiel wrote while Judah was in exile. What a remarkable setting from which to write about the possession of the land! Ezekiel broadens the concept of possessing the land/returning to the land by introducing the powerful theme of receiving the Spirit, and that linkage requires us to expand our understanding of Ezekiel's comprehension of possession of the land. In chapters 33-39 Ezekiel unfolds a broadening understanding of possessing the land.

Possession of the land was a deep and driving mission for Judah, but Judah's thinking on possession had become seriously flawed. God addressed their deeply mistaken understanding of possession in Ezekiel 33:23-29:

> *The word of the Lord came to me: Mortal, the inhabitants of these waste places in the land of Israel keep saying, "Abraham was only one man, yet he got possession of the land; but we are many; the land is surely given us to possess. Therefore say to them, Thus says the Lord God: You eat flesh with the blood, and lift up your eyes to your idols, and shed blood; shall you then possess the land? You depend on your swords, you commit abominations, and each of you defiles his neighbor's wife; shall you then possess the land? Say this to them, Thus says the Lord God: As I live, surely those who are in the waste places shall fall by the sword; and those who are in the open field I will give to the wild animals to be devoured; and those who are in strongholds and in caves shall die by pestilence. I will make the land a desolation and a waste, and its proud might shall come to an end; and the mountains of Israel shall be so desolate that no one will pass through. Then they they shall know that I am the Lord, when I have made the land a desolation and*

a waste because of all their abominations that they have committed.

Notice what contradicts possessing the land: eating blood, respecting/worshiping idols, shedding blood, depending on your swords, committing abominations, defiling a neighbor's wife (see Ezek. 33:25-26). Holiness, integrity, trust in God, these themes mark out the expanded terrain of not only the nature of the land, but how "the land" was/is to be taken/possessed.

Because Israel's shepherd had not been leaders with integrity (see Ezek. 34:1), the Lord becomes Shepherd (verse 11). *"I myself will be the shepherd of my sheep…"* (Ezek. 34:15). Notice the direct involvement of the Lord according to Ezekiel 34:12-31:

- *"I will seek out My sheep."*

- *"I will rescue them from all the places to which they have been scattered on a day of clouds and thick darkness"* (see also Isa. 60:2).

- *"I will bring them out from the peoples and gather them from the countries, and will bring them into their own land."*

- *"I will feed them on the mountains of Israel, by the watercourses, and in all the inhabited parts of the land."*

- *"There they shall lie down in good grazing land, and they shall feed on rich pasture on the mountains of Israel."* (Notice the similarity to Psalm 23.) Notice also how this is metaphoric, thus our understanding of the land.

- *"I m will be the shepherd of my sheep, and I will make them lie down, says the Lord God."*

- *"I will seek the lost, I will bring back the strayed"* (notice how the lost and the strayed now points beyond Israel), *"and I will bind up the injured"* (how this sounds like the Lord *"binding up the broken-hearted"* in Isaiah 61:1), *"I will strengthen the weak. I will feed them with justice."*

- Note in this possession theme that the Lord will set up over them one shepherd, My servant David. He, David, would feed God's people and be our shepherd. David had been dead nearly 500 years, yet God says, *"I, the Lord, will be their God, and my servant David shall be prince among them."* Of course we understand this David to refer to Jesus. Just as the land is broadened beyond the dirt in Israel to extend to the whole earth, so the term David expands to refer to Jesus. Such is the way prophecy is read.

- Now notice possession themes: *"I will make with them a covenant of peace and banish wild animals from the land, so that they may live in the wild and sleep in the woods securely."*

- Observe the intriguing term "hill." *"I will make them and the region around my hill a blessing."* Can you picture ripples of blessings around God's people everywhere around the earth? Then there are showers of blessings, harvest from trees and the earth. Note how the whole earth is this picture! *"They shall be secure on their soil."* How deeply dignifying and comforting is this hope promise!

- *Now God's people are saved from slavery. They live in safety and without fear.* That's possession of the land!

- *No longer will hunger be a problem, and God's people will have the respect of the nations.* That's possessing the land.

- The great theme which Emmanuel would declare is here described, *"They shall know that I, the Lord their God, am with them, and that they, the house of Israel, are my people, says the Lord God. You are my sheep, the sheep of my pasture, and I am your God, says the Lord God."* Ezekiel declares the great worship text for all people, *"we are his people, and the sheep of his pasture"* (Ps. 100:3).

Ezekiel chapters 36-40 describe the way in which God, through His servant David, namely Jesus Christ, and through His Spirit equips His people to possess the land/earth, via holiness, integrity, and trust in God. It's a fascinating and heartwarming picture.

When the enemies of God and His people take possession of the land/earth, the hot jealousy of God results (see Ezek. 36:2,5,6). The mountains of Israel, an interesting phrase that is a precursor to the whole earth, shall *"shoot out your branches"* (Ezek. 36:8), because God's people are seen coming home. As in Isaiah 49:8 the land (earth) is going to be restored, the desolate inheritances are going to be reassigned. Ezekiel 36:9-12 says the mountains of Israel shall be tilled and sown, God's people's population will be multiplied, towns shall be inhabited and waste places rebuilt (see Isa. 49:8). Increase, fruitfulness—these are the words used. That's the picture! Then God's people will know He is the Lord. God will lead people upon the mountains of Israel. God's people will possess the mountains of Israel and the mountain of Israel (the Kingdom of the people of God) shall be the inheritance of Your people.

While in Exile God spoke to His people through Ezekiel (see Ezek. 36:16-27). He reminded them that they defiled the soil upon which they lived, and God uses the vivid and disgusting imagery of menstrual flow as it fouls the cloth or pad or underwear of the woman. That's what Israel had done in their own land. That's why Israel was dispersed. Now the Lord describes a remarkable cleansing transformation of his graphic menstrual flow imagery. Indeed exile was not the future of God's people. Possessing of the land is their future. Now Ezekiel 36:25-27 describes the reversal of the impurity that caused Israel to leave their land.

- I will sprinkle clean water upon you, and you shall be clean from uncleanness and your idols.

- I will give you a new heart.

- I will put within you a new spirit.

- I will remove the heart of stone and give you a heart of flesh.

- God's Spirit within you will cause you to follow God's statutes and ordinances.

The expanded message upon completion of the Exile is that in order for God's people to possess the land/the earth (for indeed the promise to Abraham was that the whole earth/all peoples would be blessed and that Abraham's descendents would indeed inherit the world according to Romans 4:13) they would need a new spirit and a new heart, and with such *"you shall be my people, and I will be your God"* (Ezek. 36:28). Cleansing precedes posses-sion: *"On the day that I cleanse you from all your iniquities, I will cause the towns to be inhabited, and the waste places rebuilt"* (verse 33). (Note again the same theme as Isaiah 49:8.) *"Land once desolate will become like the Garden of Eden"* (verse 35). *"Ruined towns* [will] *be filled with flocks of people. Then they shall know that I am the Lord"* (verse 38). Dry bones will live (see Ezek. 37:1-14). God's people will be unified (see Ezek. 37:15-22). *"They shall be my people; I will be their God"* (Ezek. 37:23). "[Jesus shall be their king.] *My servant David,* [dead for five hundred years,] *shall be king over them"* (Ezek. 37:24).

Here's the picture of possession:

My servant David shall be king over them; and they shall all have one Shepherd. They shall follow my ordinances and be careful to observe my statutes. They shall live in the land that I gave to my servant Jacob, in which your ancestors lived; they and their children and their children's children shall live there forever; and my servant David shall be their prince forever. I will make a covenant of peace with them; it shall be an everlasting covenant with them; and I will bless them and multiply them; and I will set my sanctuary among them forevermore. My dwelling place shall be with them; and I will be their God, and they shall be my people. Then the nations shall know that I the Lord sanctify Israel, when my sanctuary is among them forevermore. (Ezekiel 37:24-28).

In chapters 38 and 39 and of the enemy of God's people, Gog, God assures His people, you will despoil those who despoiled you, and plunder those who plundered you (see Ezek. 39:10). And in the destruction of Gog, *"the house of Israel shall know that I am the Lord their God, from that day forward"* (Ezek. 39:22). Indeed the destruction of Gog is whole-earth in scope: *"There shall be a great shaking in the land of Israel; the fish...birds...animals...creeping things... and all human beings that are on the face of the earth, shall quake at my presence."* The destruction of Gog *"in all my mountains* [all places of my Kingdom], *says the Lord God,"* results in this, *"so I will display my greatness and my holiness and make myself known in the eyes of many nations. Then they shall know that I am the Lord"* (Ezek. 38:19-23).

God wants the reason for the Exile known, because of Israel's iniquity and treacherous dealing with God (see Ezek. 39:23). But their possession of the land continues to be God's goal (see Ezek. 39:26-29). The coming back to the land is now expanded in concept. One named David, whom we know to be Jesus, would be king. A new heart and a new spirit provided the means of the restoration. The sanctuary of God will be among His people whom He has sanctified (see Ezek. 37:28). The prophetic platform is established which allows salvation for the world to be described by the prophet while God's people were in exile. Truly there was marvelous anticipation, marvelous hope of possessing the land of the whole earth, and marvelous salvation for the people of God!

ZECHARIAH'S MESSAGE ABOUT POSSESSING THE LAND

Zechariah reflected on the Exile from the perspective of Judah having returned. His message is parallel to that of Isaiah and Ezekiel. What provides accumulating impact is that God's message through Zechariah continues to show God's people possessing the land, the whole earth. Zechariah articulates this most clearly in Zechariah 8:12:

For there shall be a sowing of peace; the vine shall yield its fruit, the ground shall give its produce, and the skies shall give their dew; and I will cause the remnant of this people to possess all these things.

With the return of the Lord to Zion (see Zech. 8:3), namely in Jesus Christ coming to earth as king, seen in the marvelous Palm Sunday imagery of Jesus on a donkey, Jesus' dominion is established:

Rejoice greatly, O daughter of Zion! Shout aloud, O daughter of Jerusalem! Lo, your king comes to you; triumphant and victorious is he, humble and riding on a donkey, on a colt, the foal of a donkey. He will cut off the chariot from Ephraim and the war-horse from Jerusalem; and the battle bow shall be cut off, and he shall command peace to the nations; his

*dominion shall be from sea to sea, and from the river
to the ends of the earth* (Zechariah 9:9-10).

Read in the light of God's people's return from exile,
we see a broadening application of what returning to the
land means. Notice the whole-earth scope of the return
from Exile, and the implicit possession language of the text.

*"Jerusalem shall be inhabited like villages without walls,
because of the multitude of people and animals in it"* (Zech.
2:4). With the reference to animals this application goes
beyond individuals to all creation. And, God is a wall of
fire all around Jerusalem, and He will be the glory within
it (see Zech. 2:5). The boundaries of national Israel are
being subsumed by larger images. Many nations shall join
themselves to the Lord, and here's that wonderful biblical
mantra: *"they shall be my people; and I will dwell in your
midst"* (Zech. 2:11).

The whole earth is the domain of God. His eyes range
through the whole earth (see Zech. 4:6), the two anointed
ones stand by the Lord of the whole earth (see Zech. 4:14),
the flying scroll goes out over the face of the whole land,
(see Zech. 5:3), the Lord's name in 6:5 is *"the Lord of all
the earth."*

The temple of the Lord, which from the New Testament we know to be the people of God, will be built by
those who are far off, the Gentiles, as we learn in Ephesians
2:13-17 and Zechariah 6:15. According to Zechariah 8:13-
22, God's people will now be a blessing among the nations,
in the same way that they had earlier been a cursing among
the nations. Truth and peace are our watch words. Many

peoples and strong nations shall come to seek the Lord among His people.

The possession theme is strong in Zechariah 12:8-9, on that day...the feeblest among the people of God shall be like David, and the house of David shall be like God at their head. Wow! *"And on that day I will seek to destroy all the nations that come against Jerusalem"* [God's people] (Zech. 12:9).

The possession of the land, now the possession of the earth, is exhilarating in scope and hope. The posture of possession requires hopefulness, perseverance, strategizing, and initiatives. To imagine that we are not to possess the earth is to have vision aborted.

So the prophets expand the term possess the land to be whole-earth in scope. The promise to Abraham is confirmed and developed by the prophets. Jesus and Paul stand upon the wealth of the Old Testament in speaking of possession in the New Testament. We have already noted that Jesus teaches that the earth/land will be inherited by the meek (see Matt. 5:5). He stands on the firm teaching of the Psalms, the meek shall inherit the land (see Ps. 37:11); the righteous shall inherit the land (see Ps. 37:29); and the prophets, whoever takes refuge in Me shall possess the land (see Isa. 57:13). Paul similarly understands the promise of possession to be whole-world in scope when he refers to the promise that he, Abraham, and by inference his descendents, that is, those who have faith in Jesus, would inherit the world (see Rom. 4:13).

Art Cooper was a pastor in Oregon, the father of a leader in my congregation. He served a village that included seasonal migrant workers. Across the years he served his congregation and his community. He worked with the laborers in the largest fruit packing company in town, and he organized what was essentially a union on their behalf. Persons were baptized by him, and he helped families get established in suitable jobs, and receive proper support. Art Cooper possessed the land.

One day I was talking with my college freshman class about the subject of possessing the land. Then I began to talk about vocation, and one of the students helpfully asked how I made the jump from possessing the land to vocation. It's a crucial question. It may be helpful to read the Thesaurus to help us get a fuller picture of taking possession: to hold, to occupy, to have, to own, to gain strong influence over, to dominate, to take responsibility for, or to take initiatives. When we think about these verbs in relation to the whole earth, what opportunity! What responsibility! God's people will possess all kinds of vocational assignments: education, law, politics, media, business, arts, care of the earth, theology, etc., because God desires His people to rule (exert influence) throughout His creation. So, God's people need to step into this assignment, this privilege, this responsibility. Possessing the land affects our attitudes, and our faith. Far different from "holding on while nervously shaking our hands that the world is getting worse," the more appropriate posture is a "not-yet-of-age" prince anticipating becoming king. You see, our biblical interpretation, our theology, determines the parameters within which our faith and obedience, indeed our imagination functions; *"according to your faith be it unto you."* The most significant impact of an inadequate theology is its too-small scope, and thus it becomes tragic. Inadequate theology/biblical interpretation never sees what might be. It's abortion, the abortion of the soaring picture of possessing the land, especially as seen in the prophets.

Why spend so very much time listing so very many Scriptures that speak of the possession theme? Because this is the soil from which dreams emerge. When it is absolutely clear to us that possessing the land is our calling, then we begin to imagine how we might do that. I saw Andy Rooney's last regular "last word" on "60 Minutes." At age 92 he was remembering a high school teacher who said he was a good writer. Those words were golden. It was enough for him to move in the direction of possessing the land.

I said that as I was finishing this book I got word that I had aggressive prostate cancer. I'll say more about that in the last chapter, but suffice it to say, I am so grateful for those who are possessing the land regarding prostate cancer, who are looking to help men survive it. And as I have been reflecting on my journey, I have thought that I want to encourage the researchers among us to go after Lou Gehrig's disease, Huntington's disease, and on and on, in a matter similar to Dr. Phil Thuma possessing the land regarding malaria, and he and Dr. John Spurrier looking to possess the land regarding AIDS in Zambia.

Here then is this enormous biblical theme: possess the land. The Church is called to possess the land. You individually are called to possess the land. Revisit the dreams and visions God has placed in your heart and mind. Picture the world as it ought to be; where do you see that it can be improved? That's likely your place to begin your journey. It will involve risk, but it is that for which you were made. Ships are safest in the harbor, but ships were made for the open seas.

Next, we add to the expectation of hope: the nations are coming to your address.

Chapter Four

THE NATIONS COME TO THE PEOPLE OF GOD

MY IMAGE OF CHRISTIANS, INDEED my self-image as a Christian, had a decided complex of inferiority. I assumed that the really important work in the world happened in Washington, D.C., Moscow, and London. Really authoritative commentary could be found in the *Washington Post* and the *LA Times*, but not particularly from church leaders. In fact I not only did not expect the world to come to the people of God, I did not expect the world to continue. The world I experienced had stories like the following:

In the last chapter I spoke of Reverend Art Cooper as one who possessed the land in Labish Village, Oregon. I received a packet of tributes that were read at his death. Frank Leon Barnes told of growing up with Art in western Oklahoma. Barnes wrote about influences upon Art and him in the days of the Dust Bowl and Great Depression.

He lived in fear of the return of the Lord, for he had not yet believed in Jesus. He reports that his dad worried a lot too. Barnes writes:

> One of Dad's famous sayings was, "The world is a keg of dynamite and someone has already lit a fuse!" He said something like that often enough to keep me in perpetual fear. I went day after day wondering when the thing was going to blow up.
>
> I was not the only person afraid. I often heard adults in the community saying all these hard times may be leading up to the end of the world. Many people believed Benito Mussolini in Italy, or Adolph Hitler in Germany, was the Antichrist.
>
> I remember going to bed at night with the wind howling outside causing the house to whistle and moan with the dust sifting in around the doors, windows and cracks. Finally I would go off to sleep wondering if this was the night the world would come to an end and I would be lost forever.[1]

Like Frank Barnes I grew up with the influence that the return of Christ was *the* issue with which one had to deal. As well, the world was in a mess, only Christ's return would fix everything. When Carol and I had three young children we desired a fourth child, but along the way we had two miscarriages. During that time one older lady in the church told us with sighing and sad words, "I don't think I could bring children into the world now, what with how awful the world is." God in His grace did provide for us a fourth child.

However, as we shall shortly see, that inferiority complex about the future is not what the prophets describe. They see "many peoples" coming to God's people. They see kings coming to the brightness of the light emanating from God's people. I can only deduce that as God's people possess the land, and do so with steadfast love, justice, and righteousness in the earth (see Jer. 9:24), that their/our behavior becomes magnetic. The Scriptures are substantially clear that we need to anticipate nations coming to the people of God. Note the following Scriptures:

In days to come the mountain of the Lord's house shall be established as the highest of the mountains, and shall be raised above the hills; all the nations shall stream to it. Many peoples shall come and say, "Come, let us go up to the mountain of the Lord, to the house of the God of Jacob; that he may teach us His ways and that we may walk in his paths." For out of Zion shall go forth instruction, and the word of the Lord from Jerusalem (Isaiah 2:2-3).

Thus says the Lord of hosts: Peoples shall yet come, the inhabitants of many cities; the inhabitants of one city shall go to another, saying, "Come, let us go to entreat the favor of the Lord, and to seek the Lord of hosts; I myself am going." Many peoples and strong nations shall come to seek the Lord of hosts in Jerusalem, and to entreat the favor of the Lord. Thus says the Lord of hosts: In those days ten men from nations of every language shall take hold of a Jew, grasping his garment and saying, "Let us go with you, for we have heard that God is with you" (Zechariah 8:20-23).

Nations shall come to your light, and kings to the brightness of your dawn. Lift up your eyes and look around; they all gather together, they come to you; your sons shall come from far away, and your daughters shall be carried on their nurses' arms. Then you shall see and be radiant; your heart will thrill and rejoice, because the abundance of the sea shall be brought to you, the wealth of the nations shall come to you (Isaiah 60:3-5).

Foreigners shall build up your walls, and their kings shall minister to you; for in my wrath I struck you down, but in my favor I have had mercy on you. Your gates shall always be open; day and night they shall not be shut, so that nations shall bring you their wealth, with their kings led in procession. For the nation and kingdom that will not serve you shall perish; those nations shall be utterly laid waste (Isaiah 60:10-12).

The glory of Lebanon shall come to you... (Isaiah 60:13).

The descendants of those who oppressed you shall come bending low to you, and all who despised you shall bow down at your feet... (Isaiah 60:14).

I will make you majestic forever, a joy from age to age (Isaiah 60:15).

Strangers shall stand and feed your flocks, foreigners shall till your land and dress your vines; ...you shall enjoy the wealth of the nations, and in their riches you will glory… [God's people] *shall possess a double portion; everlasting joy shall be theirs* (Isaiah 61:5-7).

Their descendants shall be known among the nations, and their offspring among the peoples; all who see them shall acknowledge that they are a people whom the Lord has blessed (Isaiah 61:9).

For Zion's sake I will not keep silent, and for Jerusalem's sake I will not rest, until her vindication shines out like the dawn, and her salvation like a burning torch. The nations shall see your vindication, and all the kings your glory; and you shall be called by a new name that the mouth of the Lord will give. You shall be a crown of beauty in the hand of the Lord, and a royal diadem in the hand of your God. You shall no more be termed Forsaken, and your land shall no more be termed Desolate; but you shall be called My Delight is in Her, and your land Married; for the Lord delights in you, and your land shall be married. For as a young man marries a young woman, so shall your builder marry you, and as the bridegroom rejoices over the bride, so shall your God rejoice over you. Upon your walls, O Jerusalem, I have posted sentinels; all day and all night they shall never be silent. You who remind the Lord, take no rest, and give Him no rest until He establishes Jerusalem and makes it renowned throughout the earth. The Lord has sworn by his right hand and by his might arm; I will not again give your grain to be food for your enemies, and foreigners shall not drink the wine

*for which you have labored; but those who garner
it shall eat it and praise the Lord, and those who
gather it shall drink it in my holy courts. Go through,
go through the gates, prepare the way for the people:
build up, build up the highway, clear it of stones,
lift up an ensign over the peoples. The Lord has proclaimed to the end of the earth: Say to daughter Zion,
"See, your salvation comes; his reward is with him,
and his recompense before him." They shall be called,
"The Holy People, The Redeemed of the Lord"; and
you shall be called, "Sought Out, A City Not Forsaken"* (Isaiah 62).

These texts from Isaiah and Zechariah soar with hope.
Clearly they contradict hopelessness. Clearly they contradict the view of the world that Frank Leon Barnes' father
had. These texts clearly anticipate the nations coming to
the people of God. Far from being irrelevant, the people
of God are the centerpiece of history. The people have a
reputation of God being with us; we have an attraction
and a magnetism that draws commoners and kings, indeed
nations to us.

The Christian roots of health care demonstrate this
magnetism. Christianity's founding compassion, contrary
to Rome, was a notable component. "The classical world
possessed no religious or philosophical basis for the concept of the divine dignity of human persons, and without
such support, the right to live was granted or withheld by
family or society almost at whim."[2] As time went on "many
followers of the traditional gods were turning to Christianity" because of Christian welfare agencies.[3]

Gracious, competent living, in all kinds of ways, is attractive. On a day I was working on this chapter a friend of Carol's had delivered a promised rose bush to Carol's desk at her job; it was a gift for our new home. Carol has had lots of years of experience tending roses, and in the course of the morning she showed a fellow co-worker how to trim roses. Somehow word got around the office that Carol would demonstrate how to care for roses, and she showed many co-workers how to trim a rose. In a similar way the hopefulness we display, the love and justice and righteousness we practice, the health care we provide, the homes we build, the jobs we supply, the reconciliation we demonstrate, the peace we experience, the answers to prayer we receive,—it all becomes magnetic.

Why will the nations come to God's people? What is the substance of our reputation? Ezekiel describes this substance: integrity. We have clean hearts and new spirits. This picture of integrity, clean hands, and a new spirit is described as the prophet Ezekiel gives prophetic anticipation of God's people possessing the land, not just the land of Israel, but the whole earth. God's people are known as having clear motivations and loving aspirations for everyone. During the Roman Empire, in the years of persecution, Christians had the reputation of tending the sick, feeding the poor, and comforting the dying.[4] The Scripture anticipates that reputation expanding to the ends of the earth.

God's people, in addition to living with integrity, also have a reputation of living carefully and thoughtfully. Ezekiel spends what seems like an inordinate time describing the temple. Remember that the temple had been destroyed in 586 B.C. Ezekiel is writing decades later, and is giving a detailed description of another temple and surrounding area (see Ezek. 40). His detailed description rivals the specific instructions for the tent of meeting described in Exodus 35-39, except that Ezekiel is much more expansive. Why did Ezekiel give so much description to a sanctuary? It is because now we, God's people, are His sanctuary. We, God's people, are His temple. Indeed if the people of God are going to be so attractive that nations are drawn to us, then we need to be filled with integrity; every detail of our lives and our conduct is important.

Thus, every aspect of the life of the people of God is important. No passageway in the temple is insignificant; no dimension of our life together is unimportant. No behavior is irrelevant, illustrated for example in Ezekiel 42:14 that when a priest leaves the holy place in the temple he is not to go directly to the area open to the people, but he is to place his vestments he wore into the holy place in a special location and put on other garments before going out among the people. Ezekiel is describing the temple to the house of Israel, so that they might measure the pattern (see Ezek. 43:10). Precisely. Behavior in the Church is to reflect godliness at every level. Godly behavior and behavior of integrity attracts.

The story is told of a prosperous man who started out in his youth as a poorly paid helper in a department store. One rainy day when business was slow, the employees gathered in a corner to discuss the current baseball situation. When a woman came in, wet and bedraggled from the weather, they all continued talking except this young fellow. Quickly he walked over to the customer and asked courteously, "What can I show you, madam?" He promptly got the merchandise she requested and explained its features in a pleasant manner. A short time later, the firm received a letter from this lady ordering complete furnishings for a large estate overseas. "I want to be assisted by the polite clerk who waited on me a few weeks ago," she wrote. The head of the company responded by saying that the one she asked for was young and inexperienced, so the manager would be sent instead. But when her reply came, it stated that she wanted the person she had designated and no other. So the courteous employee was sent to advise in furnishing a famous Scottish palace, for the customer had been none other than Mrs. Andrew Carnegie![5] Indeed, acts of integrity impress others.

As Ezekiel describes the temple, it is clear that he pictures the temple as the center of what is going on in the world. Consider: from the New Testament we know that those who follow Jesus are the temple of God (see 1 Cor. 3:16). Let's anticipate that the temple described by Ezekiel is an early picture of the powerful truth and new application that Paul makes: the people of God are the temple of God. Given the theme of this chapter, of the nations coming to the people of God, this temple is not merely a building. This temple is the very center of what God is doing in the world. When the land is allotted, a center portion shall be allotted as holy, and this portion shall be for the priests (see Ezek. 45:1). Picture now, we, the Church, the holy priests of God. The sanctuary, where God meets us, is at the center of the world (see Ezek. 45:2-4).

Then to the prince (we would understand that term to refer to Jesus) shall belong not only the holy district, which includes the sanctuary, but the land on both sides of the holy district (see Ezek. 45:7); it also shall likewise belong to the prince (see Ezek. 48:21). Indeed He possesses the land that stretches to the western and eastern borders of the land (see Ezek. 48:7-8). Could this be an early picture of the whole earth?

Then Ezekiel 47 and 48 follow the remarkable picture of water flowing out of the temple, and this water makes alive everything that it touches. *"Everything will live where the river goes"* (Ezek. 47:9). On the river banks of this river that flows out from the temple are trees whose fruit is for food, and whose leaves are for healing (see Ezek. 47:12). This theme is not far from the theme with which we began this chapter, that the nations stream to the people of God. Here is a picture where the nations are being blessed by the people out of whom flows rivers of living water—the Spirit (see John 7:38-39). The revelation of Jesus Christ shows a parallel picture: *"...the river of the water of life, bright as crystal, flowing from the throne of God and of the Lamb 2through the middle of the street of the city. On either side of the river is the tree of life with its twelve kinds of fruit, producing its fruit each month; and the leaves of the tree are for the healing of the nations"* (Rev. 22:1-2). Wonderfully, Ezekiel concludes his prophecy with the name of the city: *"The Lord is There"* (Ezek. 48:35).

John, in the revelation of Jesus Christ, pictures people bringing the glory and honor of the nations into the holy city Jerusalem that is coming down out of Heaven from God (see Rev. 21:10). Furthermore, the nations will walk by the light of the city which is the glory of God (see Rev. 21:23).

Now here's the connection to this matter of the nations coming to the people of God (see Rev. 21:23). The temple is now the Lord God Almighty and the Lamb, not the people of God as in First Corinthians 3:16; the city is the people of God (see Ezek. 48:35). The city has no need of sun or moon for light, for the glory of God is its light, and its lamp is the Lamb (see Rev. 21:23). The nations walk by the light of the city, and the kings of the earth bring their glory into the people of God (see Rev. 21:24). People will bring into the city, into the people of God, the glory and honor of the nations! (See Revelation 21:26.) Furthermore, in Revelation 22:4-5 the servants of God/the people of God will reign forever and ever! This message from the Lord is the same message He gave the prophets; He is the God of the spirits of the prophets. Indeed, Revelation 21 and 22 and Ezekiel 47 and 48 show a common theme. Ezekiel broadens Judah's understanding of returning to the land. In exhilarating fashion Judah will be given a clean heart, a new spirit, the divided nation of Israel would come together, and God Himself would dwell among them (see Ezek. 37:27).

Zechariah summarizes this picture of the nations coming to God's people in Zechariah 8:3-17. Note the descriptions: Jerusalem (God's people) will be called the faithful city. Old men and women will live in Jerusalem, and here it's good to be old, for they are experiencing the blessings of long life. The streets are full of the sounds of boys and girls playing. Here there are wages for people (jobs!). Here there is safety. Here there is peace. Here there is productivity and income and harvest. Here God's people shall possess all these things. Here there is truth and fairness and peace. Note what happens:

Thus says the Lord of hosts: Peoples shall yet come, the inhabitants of many cities; the inhabitants of one city shall go to another, saying, "Come, let us go entreat the favor of the Lord, and to seek the Lord of hosts; I myself am going." Many peoples and strong nations shall come to seek the Lord of hosts: In those days ten men from nations of every language shall take hold of a Jew, grasping his garment and saying, "Let us go with you, for we have heard that God is with you" (Zechariah 8:20-23).

What are the implications of these texts? For certain these texts are the opposite of hopelessness. Far from expecting things to get worse and worse, there is enormous hope that God and His ways will be so attractive that people want to likewise learn about and share in His blessings. These are remarkable images of receiving wealth, and of reigning over all other peoples.

The congregation of which I'm part traveled to Mexico, the state of Baja California to build houses for the poor. The houses were on steep hills. I was unable to drive my pickup up the steep road/street to the location of the house; my back tires just spun. In the afternoon several of us walked through a community inviting them together for some good news and a free gift. We walked on a foot bridge over a small, perhaps seven feet wide "stream" that slowly flowed with greenish water that smelled like a sewer. It appeared that open pipes ran from houses into the stream. Indeed I expect the stream was the sewer system for the community. There was no infrastructure of water and sewer in this community. Near the end of our day of building these houses one of my fellow workers asked: "Will this ever get better?"

The question, "Will this ever get better?" is an important question. The Scriptures anticipate an onlooking world drawn to the people of God as they build houses and sewer systems, as they take on new creation assignments all around the globe. This is what Abraham saw. This is what the prophets picture. This is what the revelation of Jesus reveals. Wow! Neat! Wonderful! Surely the powerful expectation of the nations coming to the people of God contradicts hopelessness.

In the second part of the book we've explored persuasive pictures from the Bible that contradict hopelessness. God rules now. We are called to possess the land, indeed the whole earth. It is a possession built on integrity and love, and wonderfully, we are to expect that as we go to the ends of the earth, the peoples of the earth shall be drawn to the people of God. Oh, imagine this! Next we consider key components in imagining life as it ought to be.

ENDNOTES

1. Frank Leon Barnes, *From Hay Creek to Heaven*, p. 71. (Copy of the two pages in Barnes' book referring to Art Cooper are in the author's files. These two pages were among the copies of the tributes to Art Cooper for his funeral; later these

tributes were sent to the author by Art Cooper's daughter; these copies are in the author's possession.)

2. "Christian History: Health Care and Hospitals in the Mission of the Church," *Christian History Magazine*, Issue 101, 7.

3. Ibid, 16.

4. Ted Byfield, *The Christians First Two Thousand Years: By This Sign, A.D. 250 to 350* (Rockville, MD: Christian History Project, 2003), 128.

5. *Our Daily Bread,* Dec. 4, pre-1994 (author's file).

Part III

Overcoming the Tragedy of the Squelched Imagination

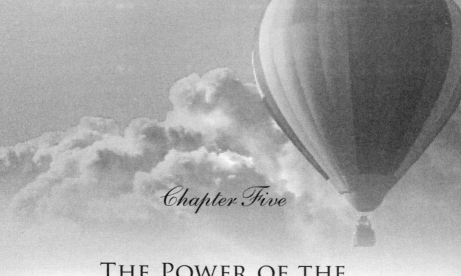

Chapter Five

THE POWER OF THE FRAMING STORY

THE RORSCHACH INKBLOT TEST WILL demonstrate your perspective: do you see a woman with a hat? Or an old woman with a prominent nose? It is assumed that one has a perspective; one will see something in the inkblot. We all have points of view, worldviews, or framing pictures. In this chapter I would like to illustrate that worldviews and framing stories have consequences. In some ways this is the major theme of this book.

Some years ago one of my distant mentors, the late Dr. Ralph Winter, Founder and Director of the U.S. Center for World Mission in Pasadena, California, wrote in an editorial of the *Mission Frontier* magazine that we should sell our libraries in order to buy Rodney Stark's *For the Glory of God*, especially the eighty pages of the second chapter, "God's Handiwork: The Religious Origins of Science." I bought the book, but kept my library. Other distant mentors have been David and Karen Mains, for many years the leaders of the radio ministry *Chapel of the Air*. They wrote two wonderful books for children (but for adults too!), *Tales of the Kingdom* and *Tales of the Resistance*. I'd like to use the work of Dr. Stark and David and Karen Mains to illustrate the importance of our framing story.

Stark makes two points in his chapter on the religious origins of science: 1) science arose only once in history—in medieval Europe (1600s), and 2) science could only arise in a culture dominated by belief in a conscious, rational, and all-powerful Creator.[1] The rise of science needed a particular framing story, a particular worldview. Science, he notes, "consists of an organized (that is, sustained and systematic) and empirically oriented effort to explain natural phenomena—a cumulative process of theory construction and theory testing" (Stark, 146).

"Many quite sophisticated societies did not generate communities of scientists or produce a body of systematic theory and empirical observations that qualify as science" (Ibid.). China had technology, but not science. "Through the millennia Chinese intellectuals pursued 'enlightenment,' not explanations" (Ibid.). Marxist historian Joseph Needham concluded "that the failure of the Chinese to develop science was due to their religion, to the inability of Chinese intellectuals to believe the laws of nature, because 'the conception of a divine celestial lawgiver imposing ordinances on non-human nature never developed'" (Ibid.).

Why didn't the Chinese scholars want to do science? Answer: "it did not occur to the Chinese that science was possible" (Ibid.). Their framing story was inadequate. "Fundamental theological and philosophical assumptions determine whether anyone will attempt to do science" (Ibid.). This statement is a key explanation of this chapter and this book. I'm emphasizing the point that if we do not imagine something is possible, we do not go there. Using the language of the title of this chapter, if our framing story is inadequate we will not imagine life as it ought to be.

Greece is a second society that failed to achieve science. They developed "non-empirical, even anti-empirical, speculative philosophies, theoretical collections of facts, and isolated crafts and technologies," but "they never broke through to real science" (Stark, 152). Why?

First, their conceptions of the gods were inadequate to permit them to imagine a conscious Creator. "None of the numerous divinities in the Greek pantheon was a suitable creator of a lawful universe, not even Zeus" (Ibid.). And when they did posit a god in charge of the universe it was an essence—it did not do anything (Ibid.). Second, the Greeks conceived of the universe as eternal, uncreated, and "locked into endless cycles of progress and decay" (Ibid.). The Greeks "rejected the idea of progress in favor of a never ending cycle of being" (Stark, 153). The concept of cycles does not predispose a society to do the work of science.

Third, "prompted by their conceptions, they transformed inanimate objects into living creatures capable of aims, emotions, and desires—thus short-circuiting the search for physical theories." For example, Plato "assigned divinity to the world soul and considered the planets and fixed stars to be a host of celestial gods." This leads away from science for "the causes of the motions of objects, for example, will be ascribed to motives, not to natural forces" (Stark, 154). The inadequacy of the framing story of the Greeks kept them from developing science.

One might think that Islam has the appropriate God to underwrite the rise of science, but it does not.

> Allah is not presented as a lawful creator but has been conceived of as an extremely active God who intrudes on the world as he deems it appropriate. ...Islam did not fully embrace the notion that the universe ran along on fundamental principles laid down by God at the Creation, but assumed that the world was sustained by his will on a continuing basis. ...If God does as he pleases, and what he pleases is variable, then the universe may not be lawful (Stark, 155).

This view is in distinction to the Christian conception of God as stated by the French scientist René Descartes (1596-1650), "who justified his search for natural 'laws' on grounds that such laws must exist because God is perfect and therefore 'acts in a manner as constant and immutable as possible,' except for the rare occurrence of miracles" (Stark, 155).

"In contrast with the dominant religious and philosophical doctrines in the non-Christian world, Christians developed science because they believed it could be done, and should be done." Alfred North Whitehead (1861-1947), British mathematician, logician, and philosopher, said in one of his Lowell Lectures at Harvard in 1925:

Science arose in Europe because of the widespread 'faith in the possibility of science...derivative from medieval theology' (Stark, 147).

Whitehead continues:

I do not think, however, that I have even yet brought out the greatest contribution of medievalism to the formation of the scientific movement. I mean the inexpugnable belief that every detailed occurrence can be correlated with its antecedents in a perfectly definite manner, exemplifying general principles. Without this belief the incredible labours of scientists would be without hope. It is this instinctive conviction, vividly poised before the *imagination*, which is the *motive power* of research—that there is a secret, a secret which can be unveiled. How has this conviction been so vividly implanted in the European mind?

When we compare this tone of thought in Europe with the attitude of other civilizations when left to themselves, there seems but one source of its origin. It must come from the medieval insistence on the rationality of God, conceived as with the personal energy of Jehovah and with the rationality of a Greek philosopher. Every detail was supervised and ordered: the search into nature could only result in the vindication of the faith in rationality. Remember that I am not talking of the explicit beliefs of a few individuals. What I mean is the impress on the European mind arising from the unquestioned faith of centuries. By this I mean the instinctive tone of thought and not a mere creed of words (Stark, 148).

I am especially captivated by Whitehead's statement, "It is this instinctive conviction, vividly poised before the *imagination*, which is the *motive power* of research." Could it be that we need a certain conviction about new creation, vividly poised before our imagination, and that such is the motive power for our working for, participating in, and looking forward to the new creation? Says Stark, "Fundamental theological and philosophical assumptions determine whether anyone will attempt to do science" (Stark, 151). These fundamental assumptions are our picture frames. Does your picture frame allow for the Lord's prayer to be answered… "Your kingdom come, Your will be done on earth as it is in Heaven"?

It is the burden of this book to invite you to reflect upon your framing story, your worldview. From the world of history, from the world of science comes this remarkable observation, that basic assumptions determine what we will attempt. Regarding the rise of science we have a prime example of the outcome of varying assumptions, of framing pictures, if you will.

What does it do to hold the vision of the Kingdom of God on earth "poised before our imagination?" Could the holding of this vision before our imagination become the "motive power" for visions and dreams, Kingdom exploits? Could we imagine Isaiah 65:17 fleshed out increasingly? Further, what if this matter of possessing a picture frame that anticipates new creation is not only a preferable individual choice that really is a better way of living, but what if this anticipation of new creation is a necessary mindset to bringing about the answer to the Lord's Prayer? What if this anticipation/faith is for the whole Church? When Jesus says, "according to your faith be it unto you," is this not an indication of the requirement of possessing an anticipation of new creation in order to see it come to pass? What if the answer to the Lord's Prayer that His Kingdom comes to earth and His will is done on earth just as it is in Heaven has a further parallel to the development of science? Allow me to use the words of Alfred North Whitehead for my own purposes:

> Remember that I am not talking of the explicit beliefs of a few individuals. What I mean is the impress on the [Christian] mind arising from the unquestioned faith of centuries. By this I mean the instinctive tone of thought and not a mere creed of words (Stark, 148).

What if the whole Church had a framing story that allowed that it could take hundreds of years for the flowering of the Kingdom on earth? According to Whitehead we have a historical illustration of this keen confidence in a God of orderliness; this keen confidence that was held for centuries, and it flowered in the rise of science.

It was Easter Sunday morning and my wife and I had just returned from a trip to Nicaragua where we met our first grandchild. When I preached that morning I said that grandparents do something that parents do not do as well: grandparents see the future in the present. Holding baby Simon I had thoughts of him being a little boy, going to school, playing basketball or soccer, being a strong young man, having interest in girls, serving God, solving problems, being a grandfather. Because grandparents typically do not have the day-to-day heavy lifting of parenting that parents do, and because grandparents have in front of them their own little babies now fully grown with children of their own, grandparents see the future.

For us the world changed when Simon was born; we glimpsed the future. Of course there is enormous work between now and the future, but in him we see the future, indeed. On that Easter Sunday morning I preached, "The world changed when Jesus came to earth." In Jesus' life, death, resurrection, and ascension He was presented before the Ancient One, and because of His life and obedience (see Rev. 5:12) to Him was given dominion and glory and kingship that all peoples, nations, and languages should serve Him (see Dan. 7:14). His dominion is an everlasting dominion that shall not pass away, and His kingship is one that shall never be destroyed.

Of course there's enormous work to be done, but Jesus started the new creation. No amount of rehearsing of potential difficulties that our grandchildren may face in the world can take away the vision my wife and I have of seeing our grandchildren entering into their world with love and hope and optimism. Similarly, no amount of rehearsing of potential difficulties abroad in this world can take away the vision of comprehending Jesus as receiving all authority in Heaven and on earth. The world changed when Jesus came to earth. This is the framing story through which we see that hope wins out over despair, and God's future may be brought into the present: everyone can get a meaningful job, everyone can have needed health care, everyone can have a suitable place to live, everyone can be safe, everyone can know reconciliation, and everyone can have an intimate, personal relationship with God. This is a picture of the Lord's Prayer answered. I ask, "Does your framing story allow you to embrace this vision?"

David and Karen Mains wrote *Tales of the Kingdom* and dedicated the book to their son in the following way:

To Jeremy

Who has the gift of seeing

As the book begins, the mother of a young boy has died. "There is a King," his mother had always insisted. "A real King." She believed the ancient tales even though signs were posted all over "Enchanted City,

There Is No Such Thing As A King,

Death To Pretenders

One of my favorite chapters is "Sighting Day."

"Sighting Day means the King takes time to play," Amanda said, turning to explain to Hero…."[2]

"The children try to find the King all over Great Park on Sighting Day," Mercie explained further. "It is a huge game of seek-the-King. He appears in disguises, and once a child makes a sighting, he can go to the practice field where the King and the children play the rest of the afternoon. Why don't you try to sight the King, Hero? (Mains, 62).

Hero had a difficult time seeing the King. His little brother had. Then, in the disguise of a beggar, the King said to Hero, "You must see me with your brother's eyes. You must see me as he sees me" (Mains, 67).

Suddenly it all came together. Hero understood. This was the King. This beggar. This peasant. This athletic young man. Here was the one who had made his brother laugh, and had helped him speak. This was the one who had poured joy into Hero's heart and taught him that games were fun (Mains, 67).

Oh to possess a framing story that allows us to sight the King doing His work in our world!

One of the assignments I gave my university class for a final exam was as follows: Write an essay on the power of hope on the imagination, imagining the world as it ought to be, reflecting on the power of imagination on action, and on Jesus' statement, "Let it be to you according to your faith." One student responded as follows:

One of the themes (of this class) is that we as Christians have in essence given up on the world. When we look around at the world's immense problems, we don't try to think of ways to reverse or solve those problems. Instead, we see it more as a fulfillment of Scripture, that the world just has to get worse and worse before God redeems it in the endtimes.... This philosophy causes major issues in the world because it leads to a loss of hope. Rather than try to make our world a better place, we simply say that that's how it is and sit back and let things grow worse. If we changed our life philosophy…we would restore hope in our lives and in the world, opening up the door for real change. Hope is a very powerful emotion. It can open up people's imaginations, allowing them to dare to dream things that they didn't think were possible before. If a person thinks that a mountain is impossible for them to climb, they will never try and never aspire to greater heights. Once hope is kindled, however, and a person believes in the possibility of scaling the mountain, they will suddenly attempt what was once considered impossible. Hope is what keeps dreams alive and the human spirit going— once a person loses hope, they lose their drive to attain a better life or whatever they were hoping for. When Jesus said, "Let it be unto you according to your faith," he was revealing just how powerful hope and faith can be. As long as we maintain hope in the power of God and faith in his promises, no mountain will be unscaleable. It is time for Christians to stop inadvertently spreading hopelessness with their complacency at the state of the world, and instead infuse it with the overwhelming power of hope that is found in God, and faith that our hopes can be realized.

Do you see how this student's framing story makes a difference? It overcomes the tragedy of the squelched imagination. It opens the way to imagine life as it ought to be.

How adequate is your framing story? Does it allow you to see hope? The next chapter provides a storyline of hope found in the Bible.

ENDNOTES

1. Rodney Stark, *For the Glory of God: How Monotheism Led to Reformations, Science, Witch-Hunts, and the End of Slavery* (Princeton, NJ: Princeton University Press, 2004), 197.

2. David Mains and Karen Mains, *Tales of the Kingdom* (Elgin, IL: David C. Cook Publishing Company, 1983), 62.

Chapter Six

TRACKING THE
STORYLINE OF HOPE

I THINK IT WAS 1992 when I made an appointment with
two friends, one a pastor, to talk with me about email.
I had heard about this phenomenon, but I was having a
hard time visualizing how it worked. Sitting in my pastor
friend's office I listened to my two friends describe a form
of communication about which I was unfamiliar. I heard
their talk, also their excitement, but I did not comprehend
what they were talking about. Sending letters across phone
lines was puzzling and remarkable to me. Not long afterward my wife needed a computer for a study course she was
taking, and gradually email became clearer to me.

Then came the language of computer storage; I was
up on them for a while: 250K, etc., though I soon lost
track of the new sizes. Along the way I encountered the
concept of opening new windows on the screen. A small

button or link on the screen led to a whole new screen with whole new links to other screens. On my BlackBerry (and I expect that someday readers will wonder at such an old machine and term) should I work only with the first screen I can quickly move between Gmail and my phone contacts and my calendar. But if I press Browser, I can then type in ESPN.com, and I am taken to a whole new world, or better, whole new worlds. I can go to the Lakers webpage, the Dodgers webpage, or to Penn State football.

The Scriptures are like my BlackBerry, in that an insight regarding a certain interpretation of Scripture can open up new vistas. I like C.S. Lewis' phrase, "further up and further in," the title of one of the chapters in *The Last Battle*. It was a place of greater insight, greater clarity, greater vision. Interpreting the Scripture includes the dynamic of gaining understanding/possession of keys that in turn unlock new rooms to explore, "further up and further in." It may be that hermeneutics, the science of interpretation, is the most important subject to master in comprehending the message of the Bible. Hermes, from which we get the Greek word hermeneutics, was the god who served as herald and messenger of the other gods.

If you identify the interpretive pattern or school of those who have taught you, you can better understand your perspectives in approaching the Scripture. A seminary professor said to our class one day, "If you will tell me the church to which you belong and where you are from I will know something about you." I remember thinking, *You will not be able to know much about me, for I am unique. I have independently arrived at who I am.* I have changed my mind since then. My professor could know about me substantially. Having grown up in the Brethren in Christ Church in south central Pennsylvania says something about me.

From those who have taught us: parents, pastors, teachers, authors, coaches, and mentors, we develop our framing story. Years ago I saw a book that studied the subject of hell. I had not studied the subject, so I bought Edward Fudge's book, *The Fire That Consumes*. How new it was for me to observe someone teaching the Scripture and coming to a different conclusion than I had previously. In those early days I hid the book in my office, not wanting parishioners to think their pastor was turning liberal because he did not believe in conscious unending torment. My framing story changed through the helpful teaching of an author. Similarly, I read Desmond Ford's commentaries on Daniel and the Revelation (both with Forewords by F.F. Bruce), and my framing story began to change from the Dispensationalism under which I had grown. Years later I was reading N.T. Wright and he commented that the Jews did not anticipate the end of the world. I was stunned. I had always anticipated the end of the world. My framing story expanded. As C.S. Lewis describes, new insight opens the doors to further insights—further up and further in— or using other imagery, new BlackBerry windows lead to additional windows which, well, is exhilarating.

In fact the genesis of this book comes out of the energy arising out of a framing story of the good news of God that is described as the redeeming of people and the restoration of the earth. (I am indebted to N.T. Wright for this phrase.) I have heard the hopelessness of a framing story that comprehends history as getting worse and worse. Jesus' life, death, and resurrection is sufficient only for getting persons ready for Heaven, but little else. I've used the phrase abortion of hope because the tragedy of abortion is that we will never know what might have been. Similarly, if we do not hope, if we do not imagine, then we do not attempt. That's tragic. Steady reflection on the Scripture, however, within a framing story of redemption and restoration is powerful.

As I write this chapter, immigration is a major issue in national discussion and public opinion. One's framing story shapes how one thinks about this subject. Cardinal Roger Mahoney, Archbishop of the Roman Catholic Diocese in Los Angeles at the time of this writing, has a framing story of this issue that begins, I surmise, with the biblical admonition that God's people began as aliens, and that compassion is the framework through which we should address this issue. So it is that he is warmly received by immigrants and friends and families of immigrants. Much of the politically conservative movement, Christian and secular, begins with the framing story of legality: "If you have papers you are in; if you do not have papers you are out." Rather ironically, though conservative Christians blanche at the thought of the mark of the beast, but with the subject of immigration I observe that fear is so strong that the principle of the mark of the beast is accepted: "If you have your legal card you can buy or sell; if you do not have your legal papers you cannot buy or sell." Furthermore, walls at the border and National Guard presence increased…these are the result of a framing story that begins with the law.

It's a fair exercise to question the internal logic of particular positions, but it is an even more important exercise to analyze one's framing story. What if we began with the framing story that Central and South America could function with structures that allow for widespread good employment, where houses were built with significant safety codes, where health care was available for all, and where violence was restrained? What if mentorship, training programs, and educational collaborations between the North and South were accelerated? Are you glimpsing how entering a new room of assumptions then has a doorway through which you see even more possibilities?

For the rest of the chapter I want to explore the storyline of hope found in the Scriptures. The accounts here are not exhaustive, but cumulatively they provide plumb lines and squares for assuring that our framing story is solid, consistent, and full of integrity. My rationale for including twenty-five texts is to illustrate the pervasive theme of hope in the Scriptures. Reading these texts is like receiving radiation for cancer, as there is a cumulative effect! The texts are in quotes, and I include running commentary throughout.

1. Says the Lord of Abram, *"I will make your offspring like the dust of the earth; so that if one can count the dust of the earth, your offspring can also be counted"* (Gen. 13:16).

2. *"Look towards heaven and count the stars… so shall your descendants be."* So says God to Abram in Genesis 15:5. That's a lot of people.

Again, *"I will make your offspring as numerous as the stars in heaven and as the sand on the seashore"* (Gen. 22:17). Dust, stars, sand. Those images are powerful. They indicate where history is going!

3. God says more to Abraham, *"Your offspring shall possess the gate of their enemies"* (Gen. 22:17). Again, this is where history is going. Pictures of a bright, hopeful future are powerful. Abraham heard God clearly, and he talked about it to his family, so that his family in far away Aram-naharim heard about it, and their blessing to their sister, Rebekah, was, *"May you, our sister, become thousands of myriads; may your offspring gain possession of the gates of their foes"* (Gen. 24:60). Indeed!

4. *"You shall be for me a priestly kingdom and a holy nation"* (Exod. 19:5-6). Spoken from before Mt. Sinai to the people of God, this Word from God defines the identity of His people. Amidst the nation-states of the world, what a privilege to have as our foundational identity and mission that which is the whole world in scope.

5. The blessings of Deuteronomy 28:1-14 are hope-filled. When you obey the Lord your God will set you high above the nations of the earth; all these blessings shall come upon you and overtake you: blessed in the city; blessed in the field; blessed in the fruit of your womb, fruit of your

grounds, fruit of your livestock; blessed shall be your basket and kneading bowl; blessed coming in and blessed going out; your enemies shall flee; the Lord will command the blessing upon you in your barns, and in all you undertake; He will bless you in the land, the land He is giving you. The Lord will establish you as His holy people. All the people of the earth shall be afraid of you. The Lord will make you abound in prosperity. The Lord will give rain in season. You will lend and not borrow. You will be at the top, not the bottom. What tremendous hope in obedience!

6. You shall be successful wherever you go as you carefully follow God's law (see Josh. 1:7). Again, what hope!

7. First Samuel 8-12 belongs with the theme of being a priestly Kingdom and a holy nation. God was not interested in His people having a king like the rest of the nations. All along He sees Himself as the King of His people, and indeed the King of the world.

8. David reflected the hopeful picture of all peoples and indeed all of creation worshiping God (see 1 Chron. 16:7-36). *"Sing to the Lord, all the earth"* (1 Chron. 16:23). All the gods of the peoples are idols (see 1 Chron. 16:26). *"O give thanks to the Lord, for he is good; for his steadfast*

love endures forever" (1 Chron. 16:34). What hope!

9. Through Isaiah God says, *"The mountain* [Kingdom] *of the Lord's house* [God's people] *shall be established as the highest of the mountains* [all other Kingdoms], *and shall be raised above the hills* [small kingdoms]; *All nations shall stream to the Kingdom of God's people. Many peoples shall come and say, 'Come, let us go up to the mountain of the Lord* [the Lord's Kingdom] *to the house of the God of Jacob* [the people of God], *that he may teach us his ways and that we may walk in his paths.' For out of Zion* [the people of God] *shall go forth instruction, and the word of the Lord from Jerusalem* [the people of God]" (Isa. 2:2-4). What a remarkable, hopeful direction of history! And when God (and His people) judge between nations and arbitrates for many peoples, notice what happens: swords get beaten into plowshares; spears get beaten into pruning hooks; nations don't lift up swords (they are plowing the ground); they are not spending time learning how to fight and defend and threaten and deceive and develop weapons that are more "effective" (see Isa. 2:4). What remarkable hope!

10. Jesus, according to Isaiah 42:1 *"will bring forth justice to the nations"*; He will not become discouraged in that process. When I first read this

with understanding I found it stunning in its hopefulness.

11. Righteousness and praise will spring up before all the nations as a garden causes what is sown in it to spring up (see Isa. 61:11).

12. Jeremiah, written as Judah was headed from their home into exile, records God's message of hope to a people in the throes of besiegement: "Jeremiah, buy a field." Recently, Carol and I bought a home, our first such venture after three decades in church-owned housing. We found God's words to Jeremiah most meaningful in that house-buying journey: *"Ah Lord God!...Nothing is too hard for you!"* (Jer. 32:17). And then, *"I will rejoice in doing good to them* [My people], *and I will plant them in this land in faithfulness, with all my heart and all my soul"* (Jer. 32:41). I know of no other place in all of Scripture where God does something, "with all His heart and all His soul." What a hopeful word to have such an intense and capable motivation and will to rejoice in doing good to us, and to be planted in the land, our place of influence!

13. As Ezekiel's prophecy concludes, he sees a river coming from the temple, a marvelous picture of the Spirit pouring forth from the people of God. (Think of John 7:38-39 where Jesus says, *"Out of the believer's heart shall flow rivers*

of living water." Now He said this about the Spirit.) Ezekiel 47:9 reports, *"everything will live where the river goes."* What hope! The pictures of hope in the Major Prophets are not ancillary. They are fundamental and foundational; these pictures are the point which the prophets are making; they are the end toward which history is going.

14. The Minor Prophets similarly conclude their writings with hope: exhilarating, necessary-to-understand hope. Zechariah knows the proper emotional response, *"Rejoice greatly!"* *"Your king comes to you...he shall command peace to the nations; his dominion shall be from sea to sea. He comes riding on a donkey"*—Jesus, of course (see Zech. 9:9-10).

15. Zephaniah 3:17 says, *God is in your midst* (sound familiar?). *He will exalt over you with loud singing.*

16. Haggai 2:7 (NIV) declares, *"..what is desired of all nations shall come."* Jesus, of course!

17. Habakkuk 2:4 trumpets in response to hard questions about where God is while evil seems to prosper, *There is a sure vision...the righteous live by their faith.* Though evidence is scant or even contrary, I will rejoice in God (see Hab. 3:18).

18. Daniel declares that in the days of the Roman Empire in Daniel 2:44, *"The God of heaven will*

set up a kingdom that shall never be destroyed, nor shall this kingdom be left to another people. It shall crush all these kingdoms and bring them to an end, and it shall stand forever." Indeed it was at this time that Jesus came into the world.

19. To Jesus was given *"dominion, glory, and kingship that all peoples, nations, and languages should serve him. His dominion is an everlasting dominion that shall not pass away, and his kingship is one that shall never be destroyed"* (Dan. 7:14).

20. Jesus fulfills the law and the Prophets (see Matt. 5:17).

21. *"Your kingdom come. Your will be done, on earth as it is in heaven"* (Matthew 6:10).

22. Abraham and his descendants shall inherit the world (see Rom. 4:13).

23. *Let us not grow weary in doing what is right, for we will reap at harvest time, if we do not give up* (Galatians 6:9).

24. *Now to Him who by the power at work within us is able to accomplish abundantly far more than all we can ask or imagine, to him be glory in the church and in Christ Jesus to all generations, forever and ever. Amen* (Ephesians 3:20-21).

25. *If anyone is in Christ, there is a new creation: everything old has passed away; see, everything has become new!* (2 Corinthians 5:17)

A mere twenty years ago I was trying to understand email. Recently the CEO of Apple Computer, Steve Jobs, passed away. He was the brain trust behind the iPod, the iPhone, and the iPad. Once upon a time I thought that the amount of change that my grandmother saw, having been born at the end of the 1800s and living through most of the twentieth century, living before there were cars, and then seeing humans land on the moon—I thought no generation could witness more change. I'm not so sure now. With computerization and biotechnology, our imagination is still challenged.

As much as we have reason to anticipate that new technological developments will ever be before us, like cars and email and iPads, we have more reason to embrace the deep storyline of hope in the Scriptures, anticipating profound and hopeful developments. I am quite aware that when a writer makes reference to current historical trends, that those specific trends may prove in the light of years not to have matured. There are, however, trends occurring in the Middle East during the writing of this book that appear remarkable. Persons who have been in power for decades are no longer in power. A generation that has been under thumb is witnessing hope for a new day. These events illustrate the potency of hope.

I read an early draft of Brother Andrew's book *Light Force: A Stirring Account of the Church Caught in the Middle East Crossfire*. He met with Muslim leaders, bringing trust into settings of mistrust. I read Ted Dekker and Carl Medearis' book *Tea With Hezbollah: Sitting at the Enemies' Table, Our Journey through the Middle East*. They went to

Islamic leaders and asked questions like: What makes you laugh? What makes you cry? Tell us about your children.

Stories in these books illustrate politically hopeful developments, in a similar way smartphones show hopeful developments technologically. The twenty-five Scriptures listed are selected to demonstrate the call to hopefulness. In the days of riding horses who could have imagined the car? In the days of the car, who could have imagined a rocket going to the moon? In the days of oppression, who could imagine freedom? In days of war, who can imagine peace? Who could imagine God's will being done on earth as it is in Heaven? The storyline of hope found in the Scriptures imagines life as it ought to be. These Scriptures are too powerful to ignore.

This storyline of hope in the Scriptures fuels our anticipation of God's preferred future. Just because email was hard for me to understand, did not mean that it was not possible. The storyline of email, on to iPods, to iPhones, and to iPads has opened us to expect developments that are not yet with us. Even more so, the storyline that God has promised to bless all the families of the earth, now with the coming of Jesus, opens us to expect developments that are not yet with us. What hope!

It's Christmas time as I conclude this chapter. This weekend my wife and I will go to the Azusa Pacific University Christmas concert, and one of the songs on the program is "I Have Seen the Light" by Robert Sterling and Chris Machen. The refrain soars:

I have seen the light shining in the darkness,

bursting through the shadows, delivering the dawn.

I have seen the light whose holy name is Jesus,

His kingdom is forever; He reigns on Heaven's throne!

We turn now to the importance of Jesus coming to earth—as a baby.

Chapter Seven

THE IMPORTANCE OF JESUS' COMING— AS A BABY

I DRAW A ROUGH TIMELINE on the whiteboard: a manger with baby Jesus lying in it, Jesus' life (I draw a line), His death (I draw a cross), resurrection (an arrow up), and then all the way to the right of the whiteboard, Christ's return (an arrow down). I say to the class, "I have always assumed that the world would get fixed by Jesus upon His second coming, and not before. However," I continue, "that view is changing." I then take my dry erase marker and walk from one end of the whiteboard to another, drawing a large oblong "circle" around the manger on the left side of the board, and the return of Christ on the right. "It's important," I say, "when it comes to thinking about Jesus that we include the coming of Jesus as a baby." That's the focus of this chapter.

I grew up with a clear view that after Jesus returns the second time He would make the world like He wanted it to be in the first place. Oftentimes this view had an element of "righteous disgust." God was getting so sick of the way the world was going that He was going to send Jesus back soon to show those rebellious hordes who were living in such an awful way just what He thought of them, and how they were supposed to live. He would show them, by golly. How many times have I heard the quip, "If God doesn't soon return He's going to have to apologize to Sodom and Gomorrah for destroying them?"

When the assumption is that only the second coming of Jesus will fix the world, when we must assume that things will get worse and worse, corollaries result. Faith often becomes privatized in this view; it can become solely private, personal, and an internal, psychological experience. Here God's interest is not reconciling everything to Himself, but saving autonomous individuals. If a person can say the "sinner's prayer," "Lord, I am a sinner; I receive You as my Savior; thank You for forgiving my sins," then God is interested in little else. Regarding the rest of the world, we're on our own.

This view of the world becoming worse can lead to fear and then anger. It's a common reality: fear leads to anger. When I think back across the years in my marriage to when anger was most often present, it centered on money, and as I reflect on that response, I think that our anger was rooted in fear, fear of not having sufficient funds. When God's people are fearful for the future, then anger easily follows. In the current era my observation is that God's people are often seen as angry, angry about health care, fearful of what health care for everyone might mean for me; angry about immigration, fearful about immigrants taking jobs away from me; angry about abortion; angry about spending, especially non-military spending; angry about the sexual mores of the country; angry about Muslims and their influence in the world.

Oftentimes anger morphs into sarcasm. "Yeah, right!" Sarcasm does not mean agreement, but disagreement. It taunts with mocking ridicule, a veiled sneer, and it implies intent to hurt. It's a cutting remark, a caustic remark, a gibe, a jeer, generally ironic. Sarcastic comments say far more about the speaker than the person or issue being belittled. I hear sarcasm far too often, and I think it is rooted in the frustration of anticipating a negative future. When my kids were small and they jumped on me and "pinned" me to the floor, I did not become angry or speak sarcastically. Why? Because I knew I would win. A simple turning of my body and I was free. Privatized religion that does not care about issues in the world, angry or sarcastic behavior—I maintain that oftentimes these behaviors are rooted in an inadequate understanding of the gospel, and especially the importance of God coming into the world in Jesus Christ.

Beyond inadequate behavior, not comprehending the significance of Jesus first coming to earth has important theological inadequacies. I call it the "Jesus is not sufficient now" syndrome. It believes the following: "Though Jesus is not sufficient for the world now, He will be when He appears again." Of course this is heresy. Any reduction of the significance of the birth, life, death, resurrection, ascension of

Jesus, and giving of the Holy Spirit is unacceptable, and as I will look to demonstrate throughout this book, unbiblical. What often follows are "motivational" threats to the Church to get the Church moving: "If the Church does not wake up, take action, etc., Christianity will be lost/Christ's cause will fail/the Church will not be able to preach the gospel." All of these threatening statements reveal an inadequate understanding of the importance of Christ coming to earth. They reveal an inadequate understanding of Christ's life, the cross, Christ's resurrection, and the coming of the Holy Spirit.

Too often the Church has uncritically applied truths about Jesus only to His second appearing, when they are to be understood as applying to Jesus' first appearing on earth. When Jesus' life is seen as a whole, however, like the oblong circle surrounding both His birth and His appearing again, His life contributes to powerful, hopeful living. I will enumerate a number of ways God is working now.

First, the rule of Christ is not only understood in terms of His second appearing, but we are to understand that He presently rules. This is the thrust of His message recorded in Mark 1:14-15:

> *Jesus came to Galilee, proclaiming the good news of God, and saying, 'The time is fulfilled, and the kingdom of God has come near* [is here]; *repent, and believe in the good news.'*

This good news of God is that the rule of God has come in Jesus, and we are to believe the good news about the rule of God. We are to believe that now.

Second, we are to pray the Lord's Prayer, and, I propose, frequently, *"Your kingdom come, Your will be done on earth as it is in Heaven."* This clearly is to be prayed prior to the second appearing of Jesus. The Amish pray this prayer daily. I recently heard a professor who is an expert on Amish life say they pray this prayer likely twenty-five times per week. They especially focus on the part, *"forgive us our debts as we forgive our debtors."* Their praying this prayer regularly opened the way for them to behave in a forgiving way at the horrific Nickel Mines, Pennsylvania, schoolhouse shooting in 2006. Similarly, the expectation of the will of God being done on earth opens the way for us to anticipate that, pray for that, and work for that.

Third, we are to understand that, through Jesus and His sacrifice on the cross (see Col. 1:20), that God is reconciling all things to Himself, things on earth, and things in Heaven. This, by definition, is happening now. We optimistically are on the lookout for this development; we pray for that; we work for that. We give thanks when we see these kinds of things happening, and we are hopeful and persevering when we do not see it happening. Clearly we expect the reconciliation of all things to God now.

Fourth, we anticipate desolate heritages being restored (see Isa. 49:8). This is also the agenda for now. Some of you enjoy restoring furniture. I've witnessed an old piece of furniture that had been painted over being stripped of the covering and revealing a very beautiful wood underneath. I've seen hardwood floors being restored to show a beautiful wood grain floor that had been hidden from sight. In another picture of making what was once unproductive

productive, I'm often surprised to see the areas that major businesses select in which to place an anchor store. After development, what was once desolate is now reassigned, it is now productive. And productive we are to be. What we are talking about is the agenda of salvation.

Paul quotes Isaiah 49:8-9 in Second Corinthians 6:2, and the day of salvation is comprised of establishing the land, reassigning what is desolate but what has tremendous potential or had a tremendous history but is now wasted. With that we invite prisoners to come out of their captivity, and those in darkness into the light. When we live this way we do not receive God's grace in vain.

Fifth, because Jesus has come as a baby, we now embrace our destiny to possess the land (see Gen. 22:17). I recently talked to a young mother who works the night shift at a nursing home, and who also is completing her RN (registered nursing) degree. She said she would like to pursue further education, getting her Master's and Ph.D. degrees. Ah, this is possessing the land! It's the mindset of doing our best. It's the mindset of investing our talents.

Sixth, because Jesus came as a baby, because He has called us to live as He has lived, indeed He has called us to live in Him, we thus embrace new creation. *If anyone is in Christ that one is a new creation* (see 2 Cor. 5:17). Everything is new, and everything has the possibility of being new. The new creation in Isaiah 65, to which I give more detailed attention in Chapter Eleven, calls us to expectation and anticipation now. Building houses is a this-world experience. Getting a good job is a this-world experience. Living to one hundred years old is a this-world experience.

Enjoying one's job is a now experience. Having blessed off-spring is a this-world experience. Having God answer prayer before we call is a this-world experience. Being reconciled with persons different from us is a this-world experience. Freedom from violence is what we desire in this world.

How wonderful and how important to reflect upon Christ's work on earth now. Christ is working, and working through His people. In Chapter Ten explains more fully that today is the day of salvation. Today God is working toward His goal. He is working toward His preferred end, His goal.

Understanding the New Testament word "end," *telos,* is important. The English understanding of "end" is often termination, a point after which something ceases to exist or function. The Greek New Testament word, however, means goal, or end to which something is moving. That's a better picture of comprehending history and God's purposes. End as termination creates a discontinuity between this world and the fullness of the Kingdom that is imported into the Scriptures, rather than exported out of the Scriptures.

My first date with my future wife was in the spring of my freshman year at college. We dated for four years and then were married. Dating and marriage have a certain continuity. When we entered marriage this was the telos, not the end after which there was nothing, but rather the end to which we were headed. We, the Church, are similarly headed toward the marriage supper of the Lamb, and there is a radical continuity with our new life in Christ now. We could picture this continuity using a phrase N.T.

Wright uses, "We bring God's future into the present." All this is powerful hope.

As I was writing this section I heard an NPR (National Public Radio) newscast on the amount of trainers needed to train Afghan persons to be able to police and secure their own future. The report highlighted the kinds of things included in the training: tank utilization and various other military components. Many hundreds of NATO trainers were training 130,000 plus Afghans. And I thought, *Oh for the day when trainers are teaching, as per Isaiah 2 and Micah 4, not how to do war better, but how to build the educational system, the housing system, the establishing of jobs, the health care system, transportation, and communication.* This is a salvation view. This is behavior that will "save" the world from death. And it will take obedience related to a faith that believes that God will bless the world. When that faith in God's good news gets spread wide—what a day that will be! In that context the old gospel song might take on new significance...

> *What a day that will be, when my Jesus I will see.*
>
> *When I look upon His face, the One who saved me by His grace.*
>
> *When He takes me by the hand, and leads me to the promised land...*
>
> *What a day, glorious day, that will be!*

I maintain, friend, that today is that day. He's looking to take us by the hand, those of us who believe His promise to bless the earth. As we exercise the obedience that arises out of this faith that believes this good news of God that He will bless the world—as God's people go to the Afghanistans of the world helping them to know the benefits of Isaiah 65:17, as the Afghans see God's people living this way and they stream to God's people requesting to know the way of this God—oh what a day that will be! What a glorious day that will be! What a day this is today!

How important that Jesus came, as a baby! This is the beginning of the hopeful culmination of our world. Our prayers are anchored in this vision of hope. Our perseverance is nourished in this vision of hope. Grace sustains us through suffering by the inspiration of the Spirit and by the reality of God's victory through Christ. The power of hope on our imagination, imagining the world as it ought to be, fuels actions of faith. *"According to your faith be it unto you,"* is fulfilled again and again in multiplied ripples of blessings. In this good news of God we bless others so that they may gain courage and insight to participate more fully in what God wants done in the world.

Some years ago I put in verse the importance of Jesus coming as a baby. The rhyme follows Clement Clarke Moore's poem, *Twas the Night Before Christmas.*

TWAS THE TIME BEFORE CHRISTMAS

Twas the time before Christmas, when all through the earth,

Big problems were everywhere, God questioned its worth.

When what to our surprise, we see such a sight,

We look in the prophets: behold, God's great might!

God would fix these problems once and for all

In a powerful and deep way reversing the Fall.

Hints and promises cause hope to arise.

Let's review these Scriptures that we may be wise.

A virgin you see would give birth to a son—

Immanuel His name, see how God's solution is won?

The government is placed on His shoulders with care,

With promises of increase and peace soon there.

A shoot from the stump of Jesse will bear fruit.

The wolf and the lamb will live together, what a hoot!

The Spirit will be placed on the Servant to cope,

He *will* bring forth justice on earth, what hope!

The Servant will suffer, will die in our place,

Bearing our sin; how wonderful God's grace!

There's a new way of change, with God a new start.

Remarkably, God writes His laws on our heart.

"I will give you a new heart, and put a new spirit within you;

Yes, it will be My Spirit, to Me you'll be true."

This Spirit Ezekiel pictured as an ever deepening river,

And everything it touched new life did deliver.

Jesus said, "Out of one's inner-most being would flow

Rivers of living water"—this is the Spirit we know.

Daniel said that in the time of Roman kings,

God would indeed set up a kingdom that brings...

A kingdom that will never, never be destroyed.

It will endure forever, with its people so employed.

Micah said this ruler would in Bethlehem be born;

What privilege, this little town's legacy now does adorn!

Zechariah said this King would ride upon a donkey.

Not a white horse, quite a twist, don't you agree?

But this donkey-riding King will proclaim peace to the nations;

His rule extends from sea to sea, to earth's farthest stations.

Twas the time before Christmas when all through the earth,

The problems were everywhere, yet God valued its worth.

The prophets did hang the Word of God with care,

In the hope that Jesus Christ soon would be there.

On that night two-thousand years ago as quick as a flash,

Heaven tore open its shutters and threw up the sash.

The glory of God shown on meadows below,

The shepherds looked up, beholding the glow.

When what to our wondering eyes should appear—

The little baby Jesus in a stable quite near.

The prophets we list, we call them by name:

Isaiah, Jeremiah, Ezekiel they came.

Micah, Zechariah a great company does call,

"The problem is solved through Jesus!" Hallelujah, you all!

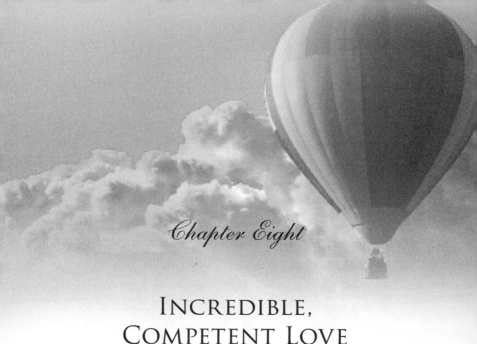

Chapter Eight

INCREDIBLE, COMPETENT LOVE

THE TITLE OF THIS CHAPTER was birthed as I read Dallas Willard's *The Divine Conspiracy*. He writes:

> God's desire for us is that we should live in him. He sends among us the Way to himself. That shows what, in his heart of hearts, God is really like—indeed, what *reality* is really like. In its deepest nature and meaning our universe is a community of boundless and totally competent love.[1]

God is at the center of the universe. He's at the center of the universe now.

My daughter showed me a YouTube clip (YouTube, if perchance it becomes out of date, is quite the rage at the end of the first decade of the twenty-first century. It's the ability to allow a huge population to see a program or video clip). This clip was of social commentator Glenn Beck. On this clip he was saying, "If your church has the words 'social justice' on its web page, run the other way." His rationale was that the social justice expectation is a progressivism that is dangerous. He said that America's founding fathers specifically believed that culture would not improve, thus the establishment of a system of checks and balances.

So do the people of God ignore the call to justice, to social justice? Not at all.

> *Thus says the Lord: Do not let the wise boast in their wisdom, do not let the mighty boast in their might, do not let the wealthy boast in their wealth; but let those who boast boast in this, that they understand and know me, that I am the Lord; I act with steadfast love, justice, and righteousness in the earth, for in these things I delight, says the Lord* (Jeremiah 9:23-24).

> *Here is my servant.... I have put my spirit upon him; he will bring forth justice to the nations. ...He will not grow faint or be crushed until he has established justice in the earth...* (Isaiah 42:1-4).

That's incredible, competent love in operation! Glenn Beck is not the only one who has thought that the good news of God should be private, personal, and spiritual. God's people aplenty have thought the same. Indeed, in the packaging of the evangelical gospel/good news (the movement from which I come) we have packaged the message of the good news in such a way that Glenn Beck would be quite comfortable. Salvation is all about a deal, a contract, a transaction based in law. It's a scene from a courtroom. It's all about you and the Judge. I can illustrate this by way of *The Four Spiritual Laws.*

I want to explore *The Four Spiritual Laws* in some detail for two reasons: first, because of the immense influence of *The Four Spiritual Laws*—the copy I have says more than a billion have been published, and second, my sense is that *The Four Spiritual Laws* as an explanation of the gospel have been uncritically accepted in the Christian community in which I have grown up. Of course, what is uncritically accepted can become a liability. These "Laws" have sin at the center of them rather than Incredible, Competent Love.

The Four Spiritual Laws begin, "Just as there are physical laws that govern the physical universe, so there are spiritual laws which govern your relationship with God."[2] That introductory statement is filled with implication, and straightforwardly it is not biblically accurate. God is not inanimate. There are not laws that are behind God, bigger than God, prior to God. God is not the servant of a giant machine of rules. These rules do not govern. The universe is not built on an impersonal, moral code which "governs" one's relation to the God of this universe. Alas, when we start here, we'll have trouble in the four laws that follow. (I have come to realize how important the tee shot is in one's golf game. If that shot is errant, then the rest of the hole reflects the reality of a whole different starting point.) How far the "laws" are from Incredible, Competent Love! No need to worry about social justice from these laws. Once the moral code is satisfied, no need to go further with what God wants.

The first of *The Four Spiritual Laws* says, "God loves you and offers a wonderful plan for your life."[3] There is good news here, but it is not the starting place of the Scripture. The "wonderful plan" of God is that He is going to bless the world. There is a world of difference (literally) in starting with the world, or starting with the individual. The good news is not fundamentally an individual matter. That individual call will come, but it's not the starting point.

The question at the end of Law One is, "Why is it that most people are not experiencing the abundant life? Because..."[4] leads to Law Two. Avowedly this is not the order or trajectory of Scripture.

Law Two asserts that humanity was created to have fellowship with God. In this sketch God is passive, unmoving. Laws are at work. Formulas are in place. A morality play has been set in motion. Two verses from Romans (3:23 and 6:23) are proof-texted to support the reason for why God sits waiting, waiting, waiting until obligations are met, until the demands of the law are satisfied. *"For all have sinned and fall short of the glory of God"* (Rom. 3:23 NIV). Actually, Paul is making this statement to put forth the point that Jews and pagans all have not initially believed in the faith of Jesus. Both Jews and pagans have refused to believe God's promise to bless the world, thus they have sinned, they have fallen short of the glory of God.

Romans 6 is not a description of a law as advanced in the second *Spiritual Law*. Romans 6 is an explanation of why and how we walk in newness of life, and not in slavery to death. Romans 6:22 is the better summary of Romans 6, (rather that Romans 6:23), *"Now that you have been freed from sin and enslaved to God, the advantage you get is sanctification. The end is eternal life."*

The introduction to the billion plus copies of *The Four Spiritual Laws* is not adequate. (The tee shot is errant.) *Law One* starts individually, not as the Scriptures do as they begin with God's promise to bless the world. *Law Two* answers a question not raised by the Bible: why are you not experiencing the abundant life? *Law Two* concludes with pictures of laws, not Incredible, Competent Love. An inanimate law stands unmovable above. A breaker of a moral code stands below. A formula to satisfy a legal dilemma comprises *Law Three*. *Law Three* pirates Romans 5:8 from its usage to answer a question not asked by the Bible.

Romans 5:8 is not a critical piece of logic in a selected line of reasoning that runs: Romans 3:23; 6:23; 5:8; 10:9,10,13. Rather, Romans 5:8 is describing Incredible, Competent Love dying for sinners, resulting in our reconciliation, and interestingly, having been reconciled, being saved by His life (see Rom. 5:10).

The big thrust of *Law Three* is that this law is the **only** legitimate law for answering the dilemma of *Law Two*. The word *only* is in bold. *Law Three* wants to assert that no other lines of philosophy and no other religion can satisfy the great moral rule in the sky. Furthermore, the progression of *The Four Spiritual Laws* is:

- God loves you (individually).

- Most people are not experiencing abundant life.

- The problem is sin.

- Jesus came to fix sin.

- Receiving Jesus is fundamentally having our sins forgiven.

- The payoff for having sins forgiven is eternal life.

- Eternal life is the abundant life.

It is ever the challenge of God's people to understand the Scripture and communicate it simply. Here is my attempt to sketch the good news of God based on Incredible, Competent Love, Jesus Christ, at the center of the universe; it makes the acrostic LOVE.

1. **Look!** God promises to bless all the families of the earth (see Gen. 12:3). He blesses the first humans upon creating them (see Gen. 1:28). He promises to bless the world (see Gen. 12:3). This promise was fulfilled in God raising Jesus from the dead (see Acts 13:32-33).

2. **Oh** believe this promise of God; in so doing righteousness is credited to us (see Rom. 4:24). We live by this faith that God is promising to bless the world (see Hab. 2:4).

3. **V**oluntarily confess your sins to Jesus (see 1 John 1:9). Through Jesus, forgiveness of sins is proclaimed (see Acts 5:38-39). Forgiveness of sins is a corollary of believing the good news of God that He will bless the world, and our living by this faith that God will do so.

4. Everyone needs to hear this good news of God!
   (See Matthew 28:19-20.)

If our summaries of the gospel are too small, too paro-
chial, too shallow, then our imaginations likewise become
too small and too shallow. Glenn Beck has not heard of
the Lord of the earth lovingly and competently working
toward fairness/justice. Though I don't know it for certain,
it seems his view of what God wants is for individuals to
follow the/a moral code. He sees "social justice" as dangerous because it has a view of history that, he believes, to be
naïve.

I have made the case that the summary of the Bible
called *The Four Spiritual Laws* is inadequate. It does not
start where the Bible starts; the Bible does not marshal its
material the way *The Four Spiritual Laws* do; consequently
The Four Spiritual Laws do not end with a picture of God
as Incredible, Competent Love.

The little *Four Spiritual Laws* booklet I have has a
yellow cover. In white letters it asks, "Have You Heard
of the," and in bold black letters, "Four Spiritual Laws?"
There you have it. One's mind goes a certain direction, and
in so doing this little booklet frames the issues, the questions, and the answers that are considered to be obviously
true. On the back page it indicates that approximately
one billion of these have been printed. That's an incredible amount. Published in 1965 when I was twelve years
old, I have grown up with them. I have used them. Forty-
five years later I am critiquing this summary of the gospel.
Oh, they "work." They are remarkably effective. They were
developed in the middle of modernity. Logic, productivity,

"if this, then that," cause and effect, rule-based, such was the world ready for reducing a library, that is the Bible, to four laws. The Church in North America was ready for that. North American missionaries exported this reduction of the scriptural library. If one agreed with the premise, the conclusion followed.

Not only did *The Four Spiritual Laws* produce the product desired, persons who assent to this line of logic and live accordingly, but it effectively hindered the Church from comprehending a more accurate summary of biblical truth.

Forty-five years later something has happened. Modernity has disappeared. The world of tight logic has disappeared. If another believes differently, the world says, "fine." Further, and more importantly, the good news of God is bursting forth from the pages of the library that is the Bible. The summary that is *The Four Spiritual Laws* is seen to be far too inadequate: laws cannot govern "your relationship with God." God is not a silent moral code who is moved like a chess piece ("Where is Christ right now in relation to you?") onto a chair in our life. These four laws make the apex of what God and Jesus are about in the world is the getting of individuals to move Christ into place so that moral failure is forgiven and moral truth is followed.

The study of the Scriptures, however, the lack of response of the children of the Baby Boomers to a modernistic description of the Bible, and the waning of the excitement of "one more" who has agreed to the logic of *The Four Spiritual Laws* has opened up whole new horizons. A more faithful starting point for summarizing the Bible is being used. A more faithful reflection on the Scripture is occurring, and consequently hope is rising.

If God promised to bless the world, and He did, and if our righteousness is fundamentally in believing this promise, and it is, and if God is looking for obedience that arises out of this faith, and He is—what possibilities arise as we have the same faith as Jesus! (See Romans 3:22,26.) What benefits to the world arise as we participate in God's blessing the world!

Steve and Chris Newcomer, friends of ours, live in the light of blessing the families of the earth. In the middle of the first decade of the twenty-first century they decided to return to serve in Zimbabwe. Years earlier they had spent the better part of two decades there. Now the country was in economic crisis, but they wanted to serve, and they wanted to be there when things began to turn around. How marvelously have they joined God's enterprise in blessing the families of Zimbabwe!

What wonderful benefits occur in places around the world as young and old alike establish infrastructures of sewer and water and electrical services. What benefit as individuals and groups reflect on how to bless a nation with dams and water conservation so that floods do not destroy as did those in Pakistan in 2010. The horizon explodes with possibilities. This active God of the Bible who promised He would bless the world has fulfilled His promise by raising Jesus (see Acts 13:32-33). What good news to declare to the world that the rule of God has come in Jesus, and all manner of exploits may be attempted and carried out based on the faith that Mark 1:14-15 is true.

...Jesus came to Galilee, proclaiming the good news of God, and saying, "The time is fulfilled, and the kingdom of God has come near; repent, and believe in the good news."

Incredible, Competent Love is at the center of the universe!

The prophets foresaw such attractiveness of the people of God that people will flock to us because we have a reputation that God is with us!

Thus says the Lord of hosts: In those days ten men from nations of every language shall take hold of a Jew, grasping his garment and saying, "Let us go with you, for we have heard that God is with you" (Zechariah 8:23).

In the days to come the mountain of the Lord's house shall be established as the highest of the mountains, and shall be raised above the hills; all the nations shall stream to it. Many peoples shall come and say, "Come, let us go up to the house of the God of Jacob; that He may teach us His ways and that we may walk in His paths." For out of Zion shall go forth instruction, and the word of the Lord from Jerusalem (Isaiah 2:2-3).

One of my Brethren in Christ pastoral colleagues is Eric Stanton. I am indebted to him for the following story. His materials illustrate the power of love in his son's life, and in core values for living. In the Spring 2010 issue of

Living Healthy, a magazine for Blue Cross Blue Shield of Michigan members, Eric Stanton's son, Jon, tells his story. It's entitled "Jon Stanton's Inspiring Story: How he lost weight, got healthy and found love."[5] Inside, the heading reads, "Inspired to change, he now inspires others." In 2007 Jon weighed 430 pounds, had type two diabetes, and was taking medications for blood pressure, cholesterol, and arthritis. It was at that time that Jon got a life-giving word from his doctor, a loving word. He said, "Jon, if you don't do something about your weight you will be dead before turning 50." Jon decided to change how he was eating, and to begin to exercise.

By 2010 he had lost more than 230 pounds, is walking and cycling, and is off medications for blood pressure, cholesterol, and arthritis. He also became engaged to be married. His first advice, "Losing weight and keeping it off is more about your mind than your body. You have to make a mental change. View yourself as the healthy person you want to be, and convince yourself that you're worth it."[6] I would use this language: know that you are loved; losing weight is not so much obeying someone's command or law as it is embracing the truth that you are loved; you have permission to become the healthy person you want to be. At the center of truth: you are loved.

TOMS Shoes has developed a marvelous business plan that has love at the core of its business practices. Each pair of shoes bought provides a pair of eyeglasses for underprivileged persons in the world. Through one of their partner organizations, Operation Blessing International, TOMS

Shoes tells the story of Angelo, a twelve-year-old boy from Peru. I take this story from their Holiday 2011 catalog.

Angelo patiently waited in line for new shoes. It wasn't until he was called up that he realized his feet would need to be measured. He tried to turn around and leave. Volunteers from Giving Partner Operation Blessing gently reassured Angelo that there was no reason to be ashamed; they wanted to give him new shoes that fit, and to do that, they had to measure his feet. Reluctantly, Angelo took off his old, ill-fitting shoes. His feet in plain sight, the volunteers saw the blisters that Angelo had been hiding.

The boy's eyes filled with tears, "My shoes are too small and it hurts when I walk," he said. "That's why my feet are like that because the shoe is too tight for my size. I can't ask my parents to buy me new shoes, they don't have money now, if I tell them it will make them feel bad. We are seven brothers—the little money we have sometimes is not enough to eat."

Whether in a business venture, or making a life choice, it makes a difference if the center of our universe is love or law. Dallas Willard is correct: incredible, competent love is at the center of our universe. That makes a difference in how we live. It makes a difference in what we expect. My friend, Pastor Eric Stanton, gave me a list of convictions about the future that is based on love, not law. Simultaneously it emerges out of the incredible and competent love in the center of the universe, and it prepares us for the content of the next chapter. Kris Vallotton has developed this list:[7]

1) I will not embrace an end-time worldview that re-empowers a disempowered devil.

2) I will not accept an eschatology that takes away my children's future and creates mindsets that undermine my legacy.

3) I will not tolerate any theology that sabotages the clear command of Jesus to make disciples of all nations and the Lord's prayer that "earth would be like Heaven."

4) I will not allow any interpretation of Scripture that destroys hope for the nations and undermines our commission to restore ruined cities.

5) I will not embrace an eschatology that changes the nature of a Good God.

6) I refuse to take on any mindset that celebrates bad news as a sign of the times and a necessary requirement for the return of Jesus.

7) I am opposed to any doctrinal position that pushes the promises of God into a time zone that can't be obtained in my generation and therefore takes away any responsibility I have to believe God for them in my lifetime.

A law at the center of the universe squelches our imaginations. Incredible, Competent Love, the living and loving God at the center of the universe, feeds our imaginations. When we reflect on this wonder, this positive and true wonder that God is at the center of the universe we begin to imagine life as it ought to be. This means, among other things, that the present time is of immense and wonderful significance. To that theme we now turn.

ENDNOTES

1. Dallas Willard, *The Divine Conspiracy: Rediscovering Our Hidden Life In God* (New York: HarperSanFrancisco, 1997).

2. Bill Bright for Campus Crusade for Christ, Inc., *The Four Spirtual Laws* (Orlando, FL: New Life Publications, 1965, 1994).

3. Ibid.

4. Ibid.

5. "Jon Stanton's Inspiring Story: How he lost weight, got healthy and found love." *Living Healthy, A Magazine for Blue Cross Blue Shield of Michigan Members,* Spring 2010.

6. Ibid.

7. Kris Vallotton, www.KVministries.com, search "eschatological core values."

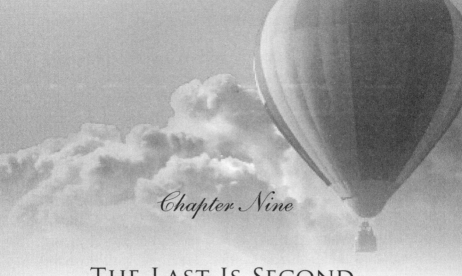

Chapter Nine

THE LAST IS SECOND, AND THE SECOND IS NOW

I was pastoring in Southern California when Y2K (the Year 2000) was anticipated. The concern was that computers would fail because they would not know how to handle the year 2000. There was a sense of anxiety in the air. Numbers of people bought a generator, thinking that electricity may not function. Some purchased food and water, anticipating that the stores could not transact business because the registers and scanners would not be able to function. We had a couple from the east in our home just ahead of that time; they had visited Saddleback Church, and were quite irate that Pastor Rick Warren was dismissive of this issue, saying straightforwardly, "Nothing is going to happen." I remember as January 1, 2000, approached, with the television showing Australia, and then moving west. I remember the celebration in London, and then New York. Nothing seemed to be crashing there, and finally here on the west coast Y2K arrived. The world did not end, nor did computers fail. Later I heard that humankind had had similar anxiety when the year 1000 arrived.

I would like to think with you about the concept of last days, and the end. I've already told you a story about my anticipation of the soon end of history when I lost my chess match after cheating on a test. I was raised in the religious milieu that anticipated the end of history at any moment. I have distant memories of checking the barn for lights (about one hundred yards away), and checking for lights at my grandparents house about a quarter mile away. I was expecting the imminent conclusion of history.

A common understanding I hear among many persons about the last days, and the use of the word *end* is "conclusion." History will conclude. "End-time prophecy" is a related phrase. Often "last days," "the end," and "end-time prophecy" refer to the rapture of non-Jewish Christians to Heaven, followed by a time of testing, and then Jewish people giving the world one last chance to believe in Jesus so they can go to Heaven, and the final return of Christ with those who had been raptured earlier, and the end of the world.

This view, like our discussion about the Four Spiritual Laws, trumps everything else. After all, what is more important than the end of history, going to be with God forever, and avoiding hell forever? Nothing, logically nothing else, can compete with this priority. Because of the apparent strength of this view it's our task to look at these concepts: *last* and *end*.

The common understanding is that the end refers to the end of history and the end of this world. Further, "the last days," in this view, refers to the remaining few days before "time will be no more." I looked up a website that has this perspective. A woman wrote in response to a blog on "The Last Days":

> I pray it all ends soon…We must pray that the Lord raptures His believers ASAP. I know I am tired of this world. I look forward to being with Christ. Please come and get us soon Jesus.

To anticipate the argument of this book, and to restate it, what a terrible abortion of hope! This woman has no hope for this world. She spends no time imagining what might be. Her faith is reduced to personal well-being, and likely getting as many as possible to assent to a doctrinal statement to love Jesus so they can also go to Heaven. She will tell them, however, that the world is ending soon.

Another woman wrote:

> Tell the world that Jesus saves! Tell the world that Jesus died for them! There's not much time left…. Come Lord Jesus come.

Another person wrote while visiting Israel:

> If these aren't the last days, I can't imagine how things can get much more dramatic.

Historically I have not seen myself in the same camp as the Millerites. (I'll say more about them in a bit.) I now think, however, that I had a view more closely aligned to them than I imagined. They picked a specific day; I did not. That's about the only difference. Because they picked a specific day for the Lord to return and world history to conclude, they ordered their lives accordingly, going to a hill to await the Lord's return. My view did not have a specific day, but the constant anticipation of the end was ever before me.

To keep persons ready for the end of history, a constant diet of impending crises are served and consumed. Here are phrases and adjectives and topics from one such website: "Frightening 150-page Report. See Now!" "Urgent." "Warning: This Report is under threat of being taken offline due to its content. It is important that you read below to know how to access the rest of the information before we are forced to take the Report offline." "Urgent. Click Here to Take our Survey, 2012 End of the World?" "Prepare for the Dollar's Coming Collapse." "Do you believe the general public is aware of the looming crises?" "Sun storms to hit with force of 100m bombs." "Israelis officially declare, 'We're preparing for war.'"

For forty years I have heard words of crises keeping one ready for the end of the world. There have been no lack of world events to keep one "Millerite" in living. Recently I read:

> "Let's pray hard, you guys, or this ship's going to blow up." That American sailor told the truth about the "good ship earth," as well as his own carrier. For our wounded world is full of holes and fire. One more global war and we shall all be destroyed.

"By 1965 we shall know if we are headed towards a permanent peace or towards a worse hell."[1]

The New Testament does not use the word *end* as we often do, nor does it use *last days* as we do, nor is *end-time prophecy* a biblical expression. Let's begin with the use of the term *last days* in the Scripture. The most significant thread begins in Joel 2:28-29:

Then afterwards I will pour out my spirit on all flesh; your sons and your daughters shall prophesy, your old men shall dream dreams, and your young men shall see visions. Even on the male and female slaves, in those days, I will pour out my spirit.

On the day of Pentecost Peter affirms (see Acts 2:15):

These are not drunk, as you suppose, for it is only nine o'clock in the morning. No, this is what was spoken through the prophet Joel:

In the last days it will be, God declares, that I will pour out my Spirit upon all flesh, and your sons and your daughters shall prophesy, and your young men shall see visions, and your old men shall dream dreams. Even upon my slaves, both men and women, in those days I will pour out my Spirit; and they shall prophesy (Acts 2:15-18).

Here the *last days* are the days of Jesus and the days of the Holy Spirit. The first days were the days of the Israelites, the Jews. They were the days when God desired through them to have His name and character revealed to the world. The *last days* were the next way that God was going to work with the world—through Jesus. There is no additional way planned. There are no additional days. This second way is the last way. It's not so much that it's near an end point as it is that it is the second way: first the Jews; now Jesus. Thus the title of this chapter: "The Last Is Second, and the Second Is Now."

Isaiah 2:2 (NIV) says:

In the last days the mountain of the Lord's temple will be established as the highest of the mountains; it will be exalted above the hills, and all nations will stream to it.

Long ago God spoke to our ancestors in many and various ways by the prophets, but in these last days he has spoken to us by a Son, whom he appointed heir of all things... (Hebrews 1:1-2).

*As it is, he has appeared once for all at **the end of the age** to remove sin by the sacrifice of himself* (Hebrews 9:26).

He was destined before the foundation of the world, but was revealed at the end of the ages for your sake (1 Peter 1:20 NIV says in these last times).

When Peter quoted Joel, Peter clearly believed that *the last days* was an appropriate description of the time. He was referring to a new afterward from the Jewish way of coming to God. This was the second way God was relating to the world; this was the last way, and the second way was now. Indeed, the last days continue.

We could use *last days* in this biblical sense if we were to say, "Air conditioners used to be considered a luxury in cars, but in *these last days* they have essentially become standard equipment." Here, as in the Scriptures, *last days* refer to two realities, a before and after, if you will. There's no sense in this usage that we mean that at any moment the world will end.

Everyone, from Peter on, needs to acknowledge that we are in the *last days*, but this is not a description of a conclusion. *Last days* are a description of the presence of Jesus. Peter and we are equally experiencing the *last days* because of Jesus.

The English word "end" in the New Testament is a translation of the Greek word *telos*. Telos is the end toward which we are going. Carol and I dated for 3.5 years prior to marriage. Leaving Carol to go home at the end of the day was one of the worst parts of dating. But on June 28, 1975, Carol and I were married. We reached the telos of our relationship. This was the end toward which we were headed. Our marriage certainly did not mean that our relationship was concluded. Rather, marriage was the end to which our dating was leading.

I remember reading one of my favorite mission texts, Matthew 24:14: *"This good news of the kingdom will be proclaimed throughout the world, as a testimony to all nations; and then the end will come."* After I had done some work on telos, end, I wondered if this verse used the word telos. Sure enough, it does. The end toward which creation was intended will result when or as the good news of the Kingdom will be proclaimed throughout the world.

Similarly, Luke 21:9 says, *"When you hear of wars and insurrections, do not be terrified; for these things must take place first, but the end* [telos] *will not follow immediately."* In fact a careful reading of this section of biblical text does not speak of an imminent end, after which nothing else exists. Follow along:

"Beware that you are not led astray" (Luke 21:8).

Do not go after any who says, "I am He" (Luke 21:8).

Do not agree with those who say, "The time is near!" Do not go after them (Luke 21:8).

Now read the Luke 21:9 text: *"When you hear of wars and insurrections, do not be terrified; for these things must take place first, but the end will not follow immediately."*

Follow the rich use of end, telos in these texts:

"Christ is the [telos] *of the law so that there may be righteousness for everyone who believes"* (Romans 10:4).

Then comes the telos, when Christ hands over the Kingdom to God the Father, after Christ has destroyed every ruler and every authority and power. For Christ must reign until He has put all His enemies under His feet. The last enemy to be destroyed is death (see 1 Cor. 15:24).

"It is done! I am the Alpha and the Omega, the beginning and the [telos]*"* (Rev. 21:6). *"I am the Alpha and the Omega, the first and the last, the beginning and the* [telos]*"* (Rev. 22:13).

Not only is Christ the beginning, but He is the fulfillment. Not only is Christ the initiator, but He is also the finished product. Not only does Christ imagine something, and begin it, but He also brings to completion what He began. This is radically different from viewing the end as returning to the nothingness that existed prior to the beginning.

Do you see how the non-biblical phrase "end-times prophecy" starts off on the wrong foot? It imagines an English definition of the word *end*, not a Greek definition of the word *telos*. End-time prophecy assumes that history on this earth is about to close, time will be no more, the earth will be destroyed, and God's people live with God away from this earth on a new restored earth. In just a bit I'll unpack some of the implications and history of such a view.

Then, there's the delightful word *suntelios*, adding the preface "with"/sun to the word *telos*. Matthew uses this word in Matthew 28:20, *"And remember, I am with you always, to the end* [suntelios] *of the age."* I am with you to the fulfillment that together we shall enjoy. It's an intensified expression of the end to which we are going. It's going together with others into the desired future that God has planned for us.

The import of this truth of God being with us into His beautiful future is thrilling. It issues forth in a whole new day. Jesus is with us into the fulfillment of the age! What a beautiful picture.

Paul Boyer, the Merle Curti Professor of History at the University of Wisconsin, Madison, wrote *When Time Shall Be No More: Prophecy Belief in Modern American Culture* in 1992. He hails from the same denominational setting that I do, the Brethren in Christ, though he experienced church life the generation before mine. He recounts belief in prophecy in modern American culture, especially premillenialism and more especially Dispensationalism.

As a historian he unpacks the remarkable influence of a kind of literalistic understanding of prophecy. In a word it expected the end of the world at any moment. It was extremely pessimistic about history now; it produced an abortion of hope.

As I have studied the Scriptures and read from outside the conservative evangelical tradition, I have come to believe that the tradition in which I have grown up has not been sufficiently rooted in the Scriptures. It thinly proof-texts, a habit for which we would criticize others. It has not understood or done sufficient critical analysis of its beginnings, and it has been strongly wind-blown by current events. The hearts of these leaders have been good. Many, myself included, have believed in Christ for salvation. Many have adopted and reflected the fruit of the Spirit.

But I have been like a chick pecking its way out of an egg. The world I have lived in has been quite small and confining. Paul Boyer sheds light on that world. There's a good reason why I have believed the history of the world to be going downhill. The preachers I heard, having been born in 1953, were reading this material.

In 1990 a premillenialist missionary in Kenya expressed her conviction that the world was growing worse as the end approaches.[2] This view that the world will end at any time gained traction by a proof-texting use of the Bible. To proof-text is to wrench a text from its context, both immediate and the whole Bible. These proof-texts were applied to ongoing current events. In this view Jesus is marginalized in the extreme. The life, death, and resurrection of Christ, the defeat of the devil, and the promise for God to bless the world have been emasculated and eviscerated. I use these words in all seriousness.

To wit, adherents of the view I am criticizing held that in the last days "conditions on earth would steadily worsen, culminating in a crescendo of disasters, both natural and spiritual. Only an eschatological event wholly outside of history—the Second Coming—would end these horrors and establish God's Kingdom on Earth" (Boyer, 66).

I referred earlier to the Millerites. According to Boyer's work, in the 1830s and 1840s, an upstate New York farmer and Baptist layman named William Miller (1782-1849) found biblical prophecy absorbing. He witnessed the battle of Plattsburgh during the War of 1812, and he ascribed the US victory to divine intervention. Later, after long biblical study, he concluded that the Second Coming would occur around 1843. He gathered this from studying Daniel 8:14. "From the early 1830s on, Miller crisscrossed the North expounding his theory" (Boyer, 81). The year 1843 came and went, and some younger Millerites settled on a new date—October 22, 1844. Keen anticipation built for that day. Devastation followed. "Our fondest hopes and expectations were blasted, and such a spirit of weeping came over us as I never experienced before. We wept, and wept, till the day dawned" (Boyer, 81).

John Nelson Darby (1800-1882) led the Plymouth Brethren, or Darbyites from the 1840s on. He wrote and preached extensively, and from 1837 to the end of his life traveled regularly outside Britain. He is particularly identified with Dispensationalism. He taught that God has dealt with humanity in a series of dispensations, "in each of which the means of salvation differed" (Boyer, 87). He taught that one cycle of prophesied events ended with Jesus' crucifixion, the next will begin with the Rapture. Current time is the Church Age, and the Bible is silent about prophecy here, "the Great Parenthesis" some call it (Boyer, 87-88).

You see immediately what the assumption of this hermeneutic does. Jesus has little to say about history now. Praying the Lord's Prayer in this system changes *"Your kingdom come, Your will be done on earth as it is in Heaven,"* to a prayer for the Lord to come again.

Somehow Darby's view of the Old Testament was seen as accurate, and coming at the same time as mounting concern among Evangelicals about liberal theologians challenging the Bible's inspiration, he was welcomed all the more so.

Darby toured the United States at least six times between 1859 and 1877, gaining many adherents in these years of convulsive social transformation. (The years in which our country experienced the Civil War.) Sir Robert Anderson (1841-1918), longtime chief of criminal investigation in London's Scotland Yard became an influential prophecy writer. James Brookes, a St. Louis Presbyterian minister, and William Blackstone, a prominent Chicago real estate entrepreneur, wrote for this school of thinking. A prophecy conference at Niagara-on-the-lake, Ontario, Canada, sustained the growing movement (Boyer, 91).

Charles Ryle, Anglican bishop of Liverpool, England, was influential in this movement. Ryle anticipated the soon return of the Lord. Given that only this intervention could change humans, he wrote that believers should "expect as little as possible from churches, or governments, under the present dispensation" (Boyer, 92). It is this precise abortion of hope that this book addresses. The Scriptures teach that we are to anticipate the reconciliation of all things to Christ, and now is the time of salvation.

Dwight Moody (1837-1899) preached Christ's soon return. A number of Bible schools spread this view far and wide: Moody Bible Institute, BIOLA, as examples. "By 1900, Dispensationalism had become a bedrock doctrine for vast numbers of conservative Protestants" (Boyer, 92). Pentecostalism, usually dated from a revival in LA in 1906, adopted premillenialism, and it viewed speaking in tongues and healing as signs of the soon coming of Jesus (Boyer, 93).

According to Reuben Torrey of BIOLA, prophecy became "the ultimate antidote for all infidelity and the impregnable bulwark against liberalism and false cults" (Boyer, 93). Moody says plainly, "I don't find any place where God says the world is to grow better and better…I find that the earth is to grow worse and worse" (Boyer, 94).

In the late 1800s and early 1900s followers of premillenialism dismissed secular proposals to make things better. "Programs of social and economic betterment by human means were at best misguided and at worst inspired by the devil" (Boyer, 95). What a remarkable dilemma, to make hope for this world to be something from the devil! Moody said, "Modern society was like a shipwreck—individual survivors might be rescued, but the vessel itself was beyond hope" (Boyer, 95). Wow! Do you see this abortion of hope?

Do not even imagine God making this world better. Do not imagine His Kingdom coming to earth and His will being done on earth as it is in Heaven. Do not imagine that at the cross the god of this world was cast out (see John 12:31). Do not imagine that Jesus made a public spectacle of the principalities and powers on the cross (see Col. 2:15). Do not imagine that the Servant will bring justice to the earth (see Isa. 42:4).

Though I was born fifty years later, I clearly heard this message. These persons just listed, who mentored the persons who mentored me, did a very persuasive job. Christians ought "not attempt in this age the work which Christ has reserved for the next" (Boyer, 95-96). This statement dare not be accepted without critique! What if the Kingdom has come in Christ as Mark 1:14-15 declares? How tragic that Christians are not praying and working for God's Kingdom on earth! How tragic, that in criticizing liberal perspectives on the Bible, these persons criticize the message of the Bible that they thought they were defending. Premillenialists did affirm missionary work. Individuals could escape this mess. They preached "not to make the world better," but "to save the people out of [the world]" (Boyer, 97).

Cyrus Scofield (1843-1921) was a towering figure in twentieth century premillenialism. An attorney (and someone ought to do a study sometime on how attorneys tend to interpret the Bible), he was jailed on forgery charges, convicted in prison, and came under the influence of James Brookes, the Darbyite dispensationalist. Three years later, in 1882, he became a pastor in Dallas.

Thirteen years later in 1895 he joined Moody's Northfield Bible School in Massachusetts. Seven years later in 1902 he devoted his full time to speaking tours, writing, and an annual summer Bible conference on Long Island. His continuing reputation rests on his Reference Bible in 1909. This work, more than any other single work, was a major conduit for disseminating premillenial Dispensationalism throughout the world (Boyer, 97-98). With notes on the same page as the text, the notes took on as much authority as the biblical text.

During the 150 years since John Darby, there have been plenty of crises to stir persons up that the end was near. World War I was one such crisis. Said one journal: "The Nations of Europe Battle and Unconsciously Prepare the Way for the Return of the Lord Jesus" (Boyer, 100-101). A.B. Simpson, founder of the Christian and Missionary Alliance Church, wept as he read the Balfour Declaration (the British document that affirmed Palestine was a natural home for the Jewish people) to his congregation (Boyer, 102). I have no doubt this was in all sincerity.

In the 1930s a genre arose that flourishes today: the prophecy novel. One such novel, *Be Thou Prepared, for Jesus Is Coming*, described the impact of the Rapture on a typical American city. Throughout this view one finds a great fatalism. Nothing can be done to make things better. A Pentecostal journal asked during the 1932 presidential campaign, "What can we do to arrest the downward current? Nothing! It is too late to patch up this old world…. Our objective is to get men ready for the next age" (Boyer, 107).

The nouns, adjectives, and verbs used by this school of thought are overwhelmingly negative and fear-producing. Bryan McLaren has said, "Eschatology always wins." No matter that the gospel is good news, the depressing language of this view overwhelms any sense of good news. Consider: "intense dread clutches at the hearts of men and women," and "men sense impending dissolution and stand helpless and impotent, overcome by the dread of threatening calamity" (Boyer, 109). "Present horrors are but the spawn to produce still more terrible anguish…. The worst is yet to appear" (Boyer, 111). Generations of people have been bludgeoned with this language. This was the ocean in which evangelicals swam. This view was everywhere.

Then, there was switching of Kingdom values to the work of the Antichrist. Anyone doing the work of peacemaking was not called a child of God (see Matt. 5:9), but an agent of the Antichrist. Truly unbelievable! These folks who had such a high view of the Scripture, and said that they did, made the Scripture a wax nose, turning it in whatever way to suit their own reading of Scripture. They were doing from one side of their mouths that for which they were criticizing the liberals for on the other side of their mouths.

Critically, this view denuded the life, death, and resurrection of Christ. Christ, in this world, only has the power to get one ready for Heaven. He merely did a legal transaction with the devil, or perhaps His Father God, to erase the penalty that would surely send everyone to hell. But for this life, Jesus is impotent. The devil is firmly in power. Any human effort to make life better here is foolish. Only the Antichrist has interest in bettering the world prior to the Second Coming of Christ.

Critically, this view works against the Trinitarian understanding of God. In this view the coming of the Holy Spirit has very little effect in the world. The Holy Spirit is not seen as God Himself present in the world. In fact, the understanding of God often comes across as the Three Bears: Papa Bear as God the Father is all-powerful; Mother Bear as Jesus is compassionate but less powerful than Papa Bear; and then the Holy Spirit as Baby Bear has the power to do occasional healings.

In 1971, shortly after Israel retook the Old City of Jerusalem, Carl Henry, editor of *Christianity Today*, announced a prophecy conference in Jerusalem. It was a stunning "success." Fifteen hundred delegates came from thirty-two nations. Prime Minister David Ben-Gurion greeted the delegates. The Jewish Symphony, along with Azusa Pacific University's choir (among others) provided the music. Speakers included a who's who of evangelical leaders. Indeed the National Association of Evangelicals (NAE), Youth for Christ (YFC), Intervarsity Fellowship (IVF), and prophecy scholars from Dallas Theological Seminary, Talbot Seminary, and Gordon-Conwell Theological Seminary were there. They agreed on this point: "the soon return of the Lord" (Boyer, 188).

These were the leaders who shaped the leaders of the early twenty-first century. They were godly, compassionate people. Many of us came to faith under their leadership. But the roots of this movement are biblically weak with regard to understanding the prophets, indeed the Bible. It is the burden of this book to respectfully provide help for understanding the good news of God as revealed in Scripture, and most particularly in Jesus Christ.

Of course the reality of the passing of time helps us. Those who spoke of the imminent return of Christ, such as the Millerites in the 1830s and 1840s were incorrect. So was John Darby in the second half of the 1800s. So was Cyrus Schofield in the early 1900s. The fatalism of the 1930s did not materialize. The end, as understood by this group, did not occur forty years after 1948, nor forty years after 1967. Hitler, Mussolini, nor any pope emerged as the anticipated Antichrist. Neither did Saddam Hussein. It is painful for me to conclude that my respected theological forebears were at sea. Their message aborted hope. Untold dreams were never given the light of day, nay never conceived, because the future was damned.

We Protestants, particularly evangelical Protestants, have criticized the Catholic Church for promoting church doctrine over the Scriptures. We have three fingers pointing back at us. We do not understand the Scriptures by and large. Many understand a system of doctrine, but that is no different from those in whom we find fault as Catholics. The young evangelicals that I see at Azusa Pacific University have been well-catechized; they have learned what we have taught them well: Heaven is the destination; hell is to be avoided. Jesus will help you get to Heaven. End of story. I have a question I sometimes ask at the beginning of the semester, "What do you find most magnetic about Christianity?" Students typically give the summary I've just given. They are glad God is gracious, that their sin won't keep them out of Heaven. But it's really hard to be passionate about that message. I remember reading the words of a nineteen-year-old student—she said she couldn't wait to go to Heaven. I thought, "What have we done to our youth?

One more word before we turn to the good news. On the morning I was writing this section I returned from playing basketball at an area YMCA. I flipped to an AM radio station and heard a preacher speaking the very subject of *When Time Shall Be No More.* Frankly it was a call to nationalism, with a bit of Jesus thrown in. The congregation broke into applause as the preacher's cadence built, "Don't take 'In God We Trust' off our coins." In the past I have affirmed such a ministry, but I am changing. As I listened to this national ministry I heard not the good news of Jesus and His rule/Kingdom, but a pep talk on keeping the US nation strong. The Antichrist received more air time than Christ Himself. This preacher's speech, along with the evident substantial following that he has, persuades me even more that the kind of thinking in this book is critically important.

One's understanding of the word "end" is crucial. If one sees this word as termination, after which there is nothing, then the Millerites become the model for living—everything is wrapped up in the getting ready for the termination of history. If, however, one sees the word end as destination, then the Lord's Prayer is our watchword, *Your Kingdom come and Your will be done on earth as it is in Heaven.* What a dramatic difference!

We now turn to the new creation that Jesus started. It all begins with a promise by God, a promise for all the families of the world.

ENDNOTES

1. Frank Laubach, *Frank Laubach's Prayer Diary* (Grand Rapids, MI: Revell Books, 1946), 26.

2. Paul Boyer, *When Time Shall Be No More: Prophecy Belief in Modern American Culture* (Cambridge, MA: Belkanp Press of Harvard University Press, 1992), 111.

Part IV

THE NEW CREATION

Chapter Ten

GOD STARTS WITH A PROMISE—TO BLESS!

BRYAN MCLAREN TELLS THE STORY in his book, *Everything Must Change*, of a pastor's son, Claude, from Burundi, East Africa, who had gathered pastors and church leaders for a conference. Claude addressed the assembly by saying,

> "In all of my childhood, in all the church services I attended, I only heard one sermon." He continued, "That sermon went like this: 'You are a sinner and you are going to hell. You need to repent and believe in Jesus. Jesus might come back today, and if he does and you are not ready, you will burn forever in hell.'"

After the group identified with Claude, he continued,

> "When I got older, I realized that my entire life had been lived against the backdrop of genocide and

violence, poverty and corruption. Over a million people died in my country in a series of genocides, starting in 1959, and nearly a million in Rwanda, and in spite of huge amounts of foreign aid, our people remain poor, and many of them, hungry. This is the experience we all have shared."

Heads nodded in agreement.

"So much death, so much hatred and distrust between tribes, so much poverty, suffering, corruption, and injustice, and nothing ever really changed. Eventually I realized something. I had never heard a sermon that addressed these realities. Did God only care about our souls going to Heaven after we died? Were our bellies unimportant to God? Was God unconcerned about our angry sons and frightened daughters, our mothers hiding under beds, our fathers crouching by windows, unable to sleep because of gunfire? Or did God send Jesus to teach us how to avoid genocide by learning to love each other, how to overcome tribalism and poverty by following his path, how to deal with injustice and corruption, how to make a better life here on earth—here in East Africa?"

Claude continued,

"Over the years, I have come to realize that something is wrong with the way we understand Jesus and the good news. Something is missing in the version of the Christian religion we received from the missionaries, which is the message we now preach ourselves. They told us how to go to Heaven. But they left out an important detail. They didn't tell us how the will of God could be done on earth. We need to learn what the message of Jesus says to our situation here in East Africa. And that is why we have come together."[1]

I made an exam question for mostly freshmen college students built on this East African account. I stated the essential message Claude heard growing up, and then I described a different essential message from Jesus, that is, the Kingdom of God. McLaren described the Kingdom of God as "God's dreams coming true for the earth, of God's justice and peace replacing earth's injustice and disharmony."[2] Then I instructed: "Describe several ways in which these two essential messages are different. Project how these two different 'essential' messages might lead to different focuses in one's Christian life."

My reflection after reading seventy responses was this: our children have heard our theology loud and clear. Getting into Heaven, avoiding hell, that is the bottom line. This is the definition of salvation. This essential message trumps everything else in the Scriptures. Protestants have become the Catholics we criticized 500 years ago for elevating church traditions over Scripture. This Heaven and hell message is not anchored deeply nor broadly in Scripture. But it has been repeated over time by church authorities. It has all the weight of influence on Protestants as does the influence of church dogma that Protestants criticize in the Roman Catholic Church.

We need to understand salvation as believing the promise of God to bless the world. *"I will make of you a great nation, and I will bless you, and make your name great, so that you will be a blessing...in you all the families of the earth shall be blessed"* (Gen. 12:2-3). One night when Abram questioned God regarding his offspring, God took him outside and had him look at the stars. "So shall your descendents be," God promised. And then is recorded Abram's wonderful response, "he believed the Lord" (Gen. 15:6). Then note: the Lord reckoned Abraham's faith to him as righteousness. Paul restates this important account. Abraham's faith was reckoned to him as righteousness. Paul makes this most wonderful further application: *"Now the words, 'it was reckoned to him' were written not for his* [Abraham's] *sake alone, **but for ours also**. It* [righteousness] *will be reckoned to us who believe in Him who raised Jesus our Lord from the dead* (Rom. 4:23-24). Jesus was handed over to death for our trespasses and was raised for our justification/righteousness (see verse 25).

"The promise" gets significant press from Paul. Romans 4 explains that the promise from God that the world would be blessed through Abraham came before the law was given. Romans 4:13 describes it this way, *"the promise that he* [Abraham] *would inherit the world"* came before the law. Again, the promise that God would bless the world came first, prior to the law. Substantially, salvation means believing the promise of God. The Bible includes believing in the One who promises, and believing the promise itself. Galatians 3:6-9 says:

Just as Abraham 'believed God, and it was reckoned to him as righteousness,' so, you see, those who believe are the descendants of Abraham. And the scripture, foreseeing that God would justify the Gentiles by faith, declared the gospel beforehand to Abraham, saying, 'All the Gentiles shall be blessed in you.' For this reason, those who believe are blessed with Abraham who believed.

The nature of the promise is that it includes a personal application to believe this covenantal word from God that when God blesses all the families of the earth I am part of that blessing. But it also includes a call to mission, for God waits to bless all families of the earth, and that places obligation and privilege upon each of us. As I embrace God's promise to bless the world, I also comprehend that gospel/good news has an "other" focus. The *"declared the gospel beforehand to Abraham"* (Gal. 3:8) is this: because of God's covenantal promise my response is to believe and receive that blessing. Because of God's covenantal promise my response is to, as I go, make disciples so that God can bless the world.

Salvation, then, is being saved from the death of living by the flesh. Salvation involves choosing life. Salvation includes believing the promise of God that He desires to bless the world. To bless others, to believe that God wants to bless all the families of the earth—that takes love. This requires the work of God in us to move us from being self-absorbed to loving others. I remember as a boy watching my mother feed scraps of food to our dog. On occasion the dog would not be hungry, and he would leave the food untouched. Should a cat come along and begin eating the food, however, suddenly the dog became hungry, chased the cat away, and began eating the food. Children can be like that with toys. Adults too, can have that same self-orientation.

We are to participate in blessing the world. *"Each of us must please our neighbor for the good purpose of building up the neighbor"* (Rom. 15:2). This is how Christ lived (see Rom. 15:3). And, we are to have hope in this exercise of blessing others. It is precisely the enterprise of pleasing our neighbors/blessing our neighbors about which we are to have hope. Says Paul in Romans 15:4, *"For whatever was written in former days was written for our instruction, so that by steadfastness and by the encouragement of the scriptures we might have hope."* This is not a text about us having hope for our future. This whole section, climaxing in the wonderful blessing, *"May the God of hope fill you with all joy and peace in believing, so that you may abound in hope by the power of the Holy Spirit,"* (Rom. 15:13), has to do with believing that God will bless all peoples of the world, with believing that His covenant to bless the world cannot be broken. As Paul says elsewhere, we are reconciled to reconcile. *"All this is from God, who reconciled us to himself through Christ, and has given us the ministry of reconciliation"* (2 Cor. 5:18). When we bless the world, we are engaging in the activity of reconciliation.

As a matter of fact, Paul's major theme of Romans 12–16 is blessing the world. Follow along; it's really quite powerful. I will track through these five chapters noting how blessing all the families of the earth provides the context for a beautiful instruction and insight on blessing.

1. Romans 12:2: The will of God is to bless the world. As our minds are renewed we do what is good and acceptable and telos.

2. Romans 12:3-8: Consider your gifts carefully in blessing the world. (Somehow I have always assumed that gifts functioned inside the Church; this is a thrilling consideration.)

3. Romans 12:9-21: What one's life who blesses the world looks like:

    a. Genuinely loves (see Rom. 12:9).

    b. Hates evil (see Rom. 12:9).

    c. Holds fast to what is good (see Rom. 12:9).

    d. Loves with mutual affection (see Rom. 12:10).

    e. Rigorously shows honor to others (see Rom. 12:10).

    f. Does not let zeal lag, with and for others (see Rom. 12:11).

    g. Is ardent in spirit, with and for others (see Rom. 12:11).

    h. Serves the Lord. In the margin—serve the opportune time, for others! (see Rom. 12:11).

    i. Rejoices in hoping with others (see Rom. 12:12).

    j. Is patient as others go through suffering (see Rom. 12:12).

k. Perseveres in prayer for neighbors (see Rom. 12:12).

l. Contributes to the needs of the saints; is hospitable to strangers; this blesses the world (see Rom. 12:13).

m. If your neighbor persecutes you, of course bless them; do not curse them (see Rom. 12:14).

n. Rejoices with the neighbor who is rejoicing (see Rom. 12:15).

o. Weeps with the neighbor who is weeping (see Rom. 12:15).

p. Lives in harmony with one's neighbor (see Rom. 12:16).

q. Is not haughty with one's neighbor (see Rom. 12:16).

r. Associates with the neighbor who is lower socially or economically (see Rom. 12:16).

s. Is not a wise guy with one's neighbor (see Rom. 12:16).

t. Does not repay one's neighbor with evil when he has treated you that way (see Rom. 12:17).

u. In the bigger picture, does what is noble in the sight of all who look on (see Rom. 12:17).

v. As much as possible, lives peaceably with all neighbors (see Rom. 12:18).

w. Never avenges oneself against the neighbor (see Rom. 12:19).

x. Meets needs of enemies (see Rom. 12:20).

y. When it comes to blessing the world, does not let evil overcome you, but rather overcomes evil with good (see Rom. 12:21).

z. In the spirit of participating in all the world being blessed, our spirit in the face of government, popular or unpopular, is to submit (see Rom. 13:1,5), to not resist (verse 2), to pay taxes (verse 6), to show respect and honor (verse 7).

aa. Owes the neighbor love (see Rom. 13:8).

ab. Remembers that all the commandments are summed up in this, "love your neighbor as yourself" (see Rom. 13:9-10).

ac. Reveling, drunkenness, debauchery, licentiousness, quarreling, and jealousy do not bless others (see Rom. 13:13).

ad. The armor of light is for the day (where all can see), so as to bless our neighbors (see Rom. 13:12-13).

ae. Puts on the Lord Jesus Christ; makes no provisions for the flesh (see Rom. 13:14).

af. Welcomes/blesses those who are weak in faith (see Rom. 14:1).

ag. Does not pass judgment on the neighbor, or despise the neighbor (see Rom. 14:13).

ah. Do not put a stumbling block or hindrance in the way of your neighbor (see Rom. 14:13).

ai. Does not agree with those who think you should put yourself first. Keeps blessing others by being alert to what they can handle (see Rom. 14:16).

aj. In blessing others (like this long list) we are acceptable to God and we have human approval also! (See Romans 14:18.)

ak. In living a life of blessing others we pursue what makes for peace and mutual up-building (see Rom. 14:19).

al. Does not let issues get in the way of blessing your neighbor! (See Romans 14:20.)

am. In blessing others, puts up with the failings of the weak (see Rom. 15:1).

an. Again, pleases one's neighbor (bless) for the good purpose of building up the neighbor (see Rom. 15:2).

ao. Christ pleased (blessed) His neighbors. He took upon Himself insults He Himself did not deserve (see Rom. 15:3).

ap. The Scriptures were written for our instruction, giving us hope that blessing the world is worthwhile (see Rom. 15:4).

aq. Steadfastness is a major discipline needed to bless neighbors (see Rom. 15:4).

ar. The Scriptures provide counsel, examples, and thus encouragement (see Rom. 15:4).

as. Living in harmony is key, which leads to us and our neighbor glorifying God together (see Rom. 15:5-6).

at. We are to welcome/bless our neighbor, just as Christ has welcomed and blessed us (see Rom. 15:7).

au. Christ became a servant of the Jews so that the promise that God will bless the world through them would come to pass (see Rom. 15:8-9).

av. God sees the world blessed, as did the prophets (see Rom. 15:9-12).

   (1) The Gentile/pagans will glorify God for His mercies (see Rom. 15:9).

   (2) Among the Gentiles praise will be sung to God's name (see Rom. 15:9).

   (3) Gentiles will rejoice with His people (see Rom. 15:10).

(4) All Gentiles/pagans are to praise the Lord. All the peoples are to praise You (see Rom. 15:11).

(5) Gentiles/pagans shall hope in the root of Jesse, indeed in the One who will rise to rule the Gentiles and in whom the Gentiles will hope (see Rom. 15:12).

aw. In the task of believing that God will bless the world through us, may this God of hope fill you with all joy and peace in believing that God will bless the world, so that in the task of blessing the world we may abound in hope by the power of the Spirit (see Rom. 15:13).

This list is how to be a minister of Jesus Christ to the Gentiles in the priestly service of the gospel of God. Yes, this is how to bless the world! This is how to bless your neighbor, such that the worship of the pagans may be acceptable, sanctified by the Holy Spirit (see Rom. 15:16). The list comprises word and deed, and includes the power of signs and wonders, all of this by the power of the Spirit of God (see Rom. 15:18-19). This is what it looks like to proclaim the good news of God to those who do not know Him (see Rom. 15:20). Again, this is what blessing the world looks like!

Note the significant conclusion to Paul's instruction: Those who cause dissensions and offenses are living the opposite of what is emphasized above! (See Romans 16:17.) People who are continually drawing lines in the sand, consistently arguing, always challenging, always criticizing, always stirring people up—they are not practicing the teaching that Paul and Christ are giving (see Rom. 16:17-18). *Such people do not serve our Lord Christ.* They are really serving themselves, and they deceive simple-minded people.

We are to be wise in what is good and guileless in what is evil (see Rom. 16:19). Namely, we are to be especially focused on the promise that God is about the covenantal task of blessing the world! We are not to become experts at evil, and get all stirred up about that. Understand this: The God of peace will shortly crush Satan under your feet (see Rom. 16:20). Blessing is the way to go. Romans 12–16 is the way to go!

Now, to God who is able to strengthen each of us according to His good news that He is about the task of blessing the whole world, and indeed its proclamation, neighbor to neighbor in the model described in Romans 12-16, *"to bring about the obedience of faith—to the only wise God, through Jesus Christ, to whom be the glory for ever! Amen"* (Rom. 16:26-27).

What powerful hope to see Claude, of Burundi, East Africa, and his colleagues preach the promise of God to bless all the families of the earth. Herein is righteousness. Herein is good news. This is the new creation Jesus began.

ENDNOTES

1. Brian D. McLaren, *Everything Must Change: Jesus, Global Crises, and a Revolution of Hope* (Nashville: Thomas Nelson, 2007), 18-20.

2. Ibid, 21.

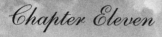

WHAT THE NEW EARTH AND HEAVENS LOOK LIKE

YESTERDAY I MET A SHEPHERD. First I want to tell you about another shepherd, Elzeard Bouffier; his story is told in an article written by Jean Giono called "The Man Who Planted Trees and Grew Happiness." Here is his story:

> Giono met Bouffier in 1913 in mountain heights unknown to tourists in a region of the Alps thrusting down into Provence, France. At this time the area was a barren and colorless land where nothing grew but wild lavender. Former villages were now desolate, springs had run dry, and over this high unsheltered land, the wind blew with unendurable ferocity.

While mountain climbing, Giono began searching for water and came to a shepherd's hut into which he was invited for a meal and to spend the night. Giono tells of his host's evening activity after the simple dinner.

The shepherd went to fetch a small sack and poured out a heap of acorns on the table. He began to inspect them, one by one, with great concentration, separating the good from the bad.... When he had set aside a large enough pile of good acorns he counted them out by tens, meanwhile eliminating the small ones or those which were slightly cracked, for now he examined them more closely. When he had thus selected one hundred perfect acorns he stopped and went to bed.[1]

Giono discovered that the shepherd had been planting trees on the wild hillsides. In three years he had planted 100,000 of which 20,000 had sprouted. Of the 20,000, the quiet man expected to lose half to rodents or to the caprice of nature. There remained 10,000 oak trees to grow where nothing had grown before.

At that time in his life, Elzeard Bouffier was fifty-five years of age. Giono informed him that in thirty years his 10,000 oaks would be magnificent. The shepherd answered simply that if God granted him life, in thirty years he would have planted so many more that the 10,000 would be insignificant.

Returning to the mountainside after the First World War, Giono discovered a veritable forest and a chain-reaction in creation. The desolation was giving way to verdant growth, water flowed in the once empty brooks. The wind scattered seeds, and the ecology, sheltered by a leafy roof and bonded to the earth by a mat of spreading roots, became hospitable. Willows, rushes, meadows, gardens, flowers were birthed. The once desolate villages were rehabited.

Officials came to admire this reforestation. A *natural* forest, they exclaimed, had sprung up spontaneously, none suspecting the precision and dedication of so exceptional a personality as the tree-planter who worked in total solitude, without need for human acclaim. Giono shared his knowledge of Bouffier's work with one forestry officer, "a man who knew how to keep silent."

Commenting on Bouffier's health at age seventy-five Giono writes: "In the direction from which we had come the slopes were covered with trees twenty to twenty-five feet tall. I remembered how the land had looked in 1913: a desert…. Peaceful, regular toil; the vigorous mountain air; frugality and, above all, serenity in the spirit had endowed this old man with awe-inspiring health. He was one of God's athletes. I wondered how many more acres he was going to cover with trees."[2]

Giono returned again to the region after World War II. Thirty kilometers away from the lines, the shepherd had peacefully continued his work, ignoring the war of 1939 as he had ignored that of 1914. The reformation of land had continued. The once near-savage conditions had continued to give way to "Lazarus out of the tombs." Eight years later the whole countryside glowed with health and prosperity.

On the site of the ruins I had seen in 1913 now stand neat farms…. The old streams, fed by the rains and snows that the forest conserves, are flowing again…. Little by little the villages have been rebuilt. People from the plains, where land is costly, have settled here, bringing youth, motion, the spirit of adventure. Along the roads you meet hearty men and women, boys and girls who understand laughter and have recovered a taste for picnics. Counting the former population, unrecognizable now that they live in comfort, more than 10,000 people owe their happiness to Elzeard Bouffier.[3]

As I said, I met a modern-day shepherd yesterday, and I'll tell you about his story near the end of this chapter.

Most persons who hear Paul say, "Anyone who is in Christ is a new creation; the old has passed away, the new has come," take his statement at face value. When we receive Christ we become a new creation. Never mind that the person is not yet mature; she is a new creation. A well-loved bishop in our church told this story: He, the bishop, was attending the baptism of a young man who had recently received Christ as Lord. He was, in fact, a new creation in Christ. The water was cold at the outdoor setting, and as the young fellow raised up from the water after being immersed he exclaimed in a voice loud enough to be heard, "Damn, that water's cold!" And the bishop paused and smiled broadly while his audience took in this story: the church was obediently making disciples of Jesus Christ, reaching those who were previously uninitiated in the ways of God. Despite the immaturity, no one denies that the young man was a new creation in Christ.

That flexibility in understanding the term new creation in Christ is also helpful in understanding Isaiah's picture of new heavens and new earth (see Isa. 65:17-25). Let's approach this text with a "what if" perspective, thinking, "What if we saw the new heavens and new earth as connected to becoming a new creation in Christ?" What if we allowed for the work of the Spirit now to be doing new heavens and new earth work, akin to the young man being a new creation in Christ, though there were some aspects of his life that were not fully so? Actually, as we hear the descriptions of the new heavens and earth in Isaiah 65, they sound very "this-worldly."

There are a dozen descriptions of the new heavens and new earth in Isaiah 65:17. First, the new heavens and new earth overtake the former things (see Isa. 65:17). The children who were playing by the stream in their vibrant village had no idea that a generation prior the place was barren. The babbling brook, the splashes of happy children, the chirping of birds, the explosion of flowers, the satisfaction of a functioning and productive village fully engages the residents. Other than for historical purposes the former things are forgotten.

Second, God wants us to forever celebrate His ongoing creative work (see Isa. 65:18-19). He is creating His people as a joy and delight; God Himself is "joying" in and delighting in us. How different is the reputation of the church at large, that we are bigoted and hateful. The "shepherd" to whom I refer at the outset of this chapter has coined a term "born against." He wants us, as God does, to be born again; we are to be known for joy and optimism, not known for what we oppose. Oh to step into the people God is creating us to be—a fun people! Well do I remember how keenly our children observed whether people we were visiting, or pastors of other churches we were visiting on vacation, were fun people or not. If the persons were fun, the children were up for the new adventure. What value to cooperate with and take on the agenda of the Spirit as He is creating us as a joy and a delight, with God rejoicing and delighting in us. How wonderful!

Third, we look to eliminate distress (see Isa. 65:19). The prophet anticipates no sound of weeping or cry of distress. Just as the description of delight is ongoing in creation, so the elimination of cries of distress and sounds of weeping is an ongoing work of God's new creation. We know what makes for joy, and we know what makes for distress. As we are in Christ and as we are new creations, we work for the elimination of psychological distress, relational distress, financial distress, spiritual distress, and physical distress. Pain and discomfort are accurate indications of an area that needs our attention.

Our son and daughter-in-law lived in Nicaragua for four years and washed their clothes by hand. They did so because they wanted to live as their neighbors did, and they did not have washing machines. They spoke of the substantial time it took to wash clothes, and especially when their son was born. Is it not fair to say that a washing machine eliminates distress? Think about the accumulation of distress that is avoided by not having to wash clothes by hand. That illustration can be multiplied in lots of ways. I don't have to carry water. I have prompt medical attention to thwart an illness that otherwise could mushroom in multiplied problems. I have had the benefit of training in literacy, and thus I can navigate this culture. There's distress to have to wash my clothes by hand, carry my water, live without medical care, or live without being able to read. What a vast and wonderful agenda to work toward and anticipate not hearing weeping and cries of distress because God's delightful rule is spreading.

The fourth marker of new creation is found in Isaiah 65:20,22:

> *No more shall there be in it an infant that lives but a few days, or an old person who does not live out a lifetime; for one who dies at a hundred years will be considered a youth, and one who falls short of a hundred years will be considered accursed. ...for like the days of a tree shall the days of my people be....*

Health care is available to all. Truly health care is a privilege. My son contracted appendicitis while living in Nicaragua. He received wonderful medical care for this life-threatening illness. His doctor told him, "My friend, you were near death." Not long after that incident one of my son's seminary students similarly contracted appendicitis, and either because he was not near medical assistance, or he could not afford medical care, this student died. How tragic! Both men are equally valuable in the sight of God, but because one had access to health care one is able to, Lord willing, live out a lifetime into old age.

The fifth description of new heavens and a new earth is this: home ownership is available to all (see Isa. 65:21, 22). This prophetic picture has echoes today in the work of Habitat for Humanity: one works on the house putting a certain number of "sweat-equity" hours, and then, privilege of privileges, that one gets to live in the house. Specifically this is not a scenario where you are a laborer, building houses, but not having the privilege to live in it. Home ownership is not so much the American dream as it is the Kingdom of God dream.

There is a certain dignity in home ownership. "60 Minutes" had a segment on homelessness recently, and they talked with children who were currently experiencing this. The children described the embarrassment of having others discover they were living in a car, or washing up in the bathroom of a Walmart. With tears emerging at the corners of their eyes some described the pain and compassion they felt on behalf of their parents who were unable to secure or pay for housing. Some described their gratitude for neighbors taking them in, or perhaps kind-hearted strangers, and they told how they did not want to go to the bathroom at night and perhaps wake up their hosts and make them upset, and then perhaps send them out to the street again. In the Kingdom, home ownership is the norm. Everyone has a safe place to come to at nighttime.

The sixth description of new heavens and a new earth is this, *"They shall plant vineyards and eat their fruit. ...they shall not plant and another eat"* (Isa. 65:21-22). Entrepreneurship is the privilege of everyone. This is not the picture of the migrant worker. The migrant worker plants and tills and picks and boxes and delivers to the store; the owner gets the return and eats both the produce and the profit from the produce. No, in the Kingdom, in the new heavens and new earth the picture is that of the entrepreneur who both plants and eats. In the new earth it is one's privilege to start a business, and live off of that business. Indeed, because this is the picture of creation as it ought to be, we appropriately can be using this picture as a model for how we might live. It is our privilege to take the assets of personality, the gifts of personality provided by the Spirit, and plant expecting to eat from the fruit of our investment.

There's tremendous empowerment here. Dr. Scott Todd, of Compassion International, writes in the book *Poverty* of the opposite of the empowerment described in the new creation. He quotes Compassion President Dr. Wes Stafford:

> At its very core, poverty is a mindset that goes far beyond the tragic circumstances. It is the cruel, destructive message that gets whispered into the ears of millions by the enemy Satan himself, "Give up! You don't matter. Nobody cares about you. Look around you: Things are terrible. Always have been, always will be. Think back. Your grandfather

was a failure. Your parents couldn't protect or take care of you. Now it's your turn. You, too, will fail. So just give up![4]

Dr. Todd then reflects,

When a child (or adult) believes that lie, then he is poor. Poverty described in these terms is primarily an internal condition resulting from an external message of oppression. The internal condition is one of disempowerment, fatalism, hopelessness and lack of initiative.... They do not make the effort of striving, risking, and capitalizing on opportunities.[5]

Isaiah pictures the new creation full of entrepreneurship; it pictures persons who are striving, risking, and capitalizing in the planting of vineyards.

The seventh description of new creation is enjoyable, meaningful jobs held over time. Doesn't this list sound like the agenda of political parties and campaigns? Health care, housing, and jobs. *"My chosen shall long enjoy the work of their hands. They shall not labor in vain"* (Isa. 65:22d,23a).

Some years ago a cynical country western song made its rounds, "Take this job and shove it" New creation is far from that. It pictures enjoyable work, work that almost seems like play because you enjoy what you are doing. It pictures meaningful work (not laboring in vain), work that has dignity, and contributes to the world working well. What a vision! For some time Zimbabwe had an incomprehensible 80 percent unemployment. This morning I heard that California has an unemployment rate of just less than 12 percent. No employment and underemployment drain life. From America to Zimbabwe this picture of enjoyable and meaningful work over time in the new creation is one of the most attractive in the list of descriptions. What a deeply satisfying picture to wake up each day having work and enjoying our work.

The eighth description of the new creation is this: healthy family systems. *"They shall not…bear children for calamity, for they shall be offspring blessed by the Lord— and their descendants as well"* (Isa. 65:23). My mother sometimes commented that her story of coming to faith in Christ was not dramatic. She came from a heritage of stable family systems so that she grew up in the disciplines of grace. Conversion for her had to do with confirming for herself theology and behavior that she had witnessed from her earliest days.

What is not so readily observed in the kind of faith story that my mother has is the marvelous asset of accumulated grace and wisdom. Though not as arresting when telling one's story, the long models of maturity, and the consistent training in godliness from earliest years are of immeasurable value. New creation pictures this transfer of accumulating wholeness. What far-reaching implications! What far-reaching stories!

Number nine, *"Before they call I will answer, while they are yet speaking I will hear"* (Isa. 65:24). What remarkable spiritual intimacy! This is the nature of new creation in Christ. You've heard of the phrase, "preemptive strikes." That's when an entity attacks an enemy/opponent first before the enemy/opponent attacks. Here God answers before we express the need. In fact He may be solving problems before they become problems—preemptive blessings.

There is an immediacy of presence that is noteworthy, "While they are speaking I will hear." Waiting constitutes a substantial portion of life: waiting to hear about a job, waiting to get pregnant, waiting for the child to be born, waiting to get the results back on a medical test, waiting for a person to retire…. In all of this and more, life in the new creation includes God hearing us even as we are speaking.

A Roman soldier leader had a highly valued slave who was ill and close to death. Through friends the centurion said to Jesus, "Lord, do not trouble yourself, for I am not worthy to have you come under my roof; therefore I did not presume to come to you. Only speak the word, and let my servant be healed. …When those who had been sent returned to the house, they found the slave in good health" (Luke 7:6-7,10). This is the picture of new creation that Isaiah paints. This sense of preemptive care is immensely comforting. We are heard, and God is anticipating what we are facing, and is working on our behalf! He's got our back, but perhaps more accurately He has our front.

The tenth description of the new heavens and earth is surprising reconciliation: the wolf and the lamb shall feed together, and the lion shall eat straw like the ox (see Isa. 65:25). A wolf and a lamb eating together? A lion eating straw like an ox, rather than eating the ox?

The last story of this book comes out of South Africa. Apartheid was the official policy starting in 1950 of strict racial segregation and discrimination against nonwhites. It was a deep, influential practice, but in 1991 apartheid ended. Now whites and nonwhites can and do eat together. New creation has a foothold in the demise of apartheid. The picture of new creation includes surprising reconciliation.

Can we imagine (and these pairs will change over the years) these groups eating together? North and South Ireland, North and South Korea, Japan and Korea, Highlanders and Lowlanders of New Guinea, Israelis and Palestinians, Indians and Pakistanis, Muslims and Christians, Mormons and Evangelicals, Democrats and Republicans, liberals and conservatives, Protestants and Catholics?

The picture of the new creation is that we are to expect surprising reconciliation. Perhaps the key here is that we ought to expect this to occur, and thus we ought to work for it, for it is an agenda of the Kingdom. When you read the last story you will say, "If this kind of reconciliation can happen in South Africa, then reconciliation can happen anywhere."

Description eleven of the new creation is profound. Evil is not elevated or elevating. The devil shall grovel in the dust. New creation clearly pictures the victory of God, of good over evil. The lion becomes a vegetarian, and the serpent eats dust. We use that phrase "in the dust" in a variety of settings: the winning car left the other race cars "in the dust"; anyone who did a project slowly, in contrast to one who did the project quickly, "was left in the dust." Enemies may be reconciled, a lion can now relate peaceably to an ox, for example. But evil's food is the dust.

Evil is not glorified. Evil is not imagined as a near-rival power to God. The serpent—its food shall be dust. The following phrases are eliminated in new creation living:

- Satan is ruling the world now.

- Satan is winning.

- Satan is all-powerful.

No, in the new creation Satan eats the dust!

Finally, the twelfth description of the new heavens and new earth says, *"They shall not hurt or destroy on all my holy mountain," says the Lord* (Isa. 65:25). Here is a picture of no violence. In the new heavens and earth, on all God's holy mountain—His Kingdom, there will not be spousal abuse, child abuse, sexual abuse, psychological abuse, trafficking of women, drone attacks, cluster bombs, home invasion robberies, drive-by shootings, gang violence, murder, rape, bullying, or insults.

Our evening newscasts are filled with such reports. I picked up the July 22, 2011 issue (as I write) of the *LA Times* newspaper. On the front page I see, "In Punjab, Pakistan a hard-line student group uses violence to enforce its fundamentalist goals." The article said that in the dead of night they showed up at a men's dormitory armed with wooden sticks and bicycle chains. One was pistol-whipped and hit on the head with a brick. This is not the way of the Kingdom, of the new creation. *"They shall not hurt or destroy on all My holy mountain," says the Lord* (Isa. 65:25).

Remember the story from the bishop about the new creation in Christ and his baptism? We allow for more and less when it comes to evidences of new creation understandings and new creation lifestyle in the individual. I believe our thinking about Isaiah's picture of new creation could similarly be understood, in terms of more and less. Theoretically evidences of new creation should be more in evidence in the congregation that I pastor, or the Christian university where I teach, than say in the prison in my city, though we well can expect that there are evidences of new creation behaviors in the prison also.

Rather than thinking that new creation is only a subject for consideration after Jesus appears the second time, that it's only a description for then, what if we make this agenda ours because this is the kind of living Jesus is looking for on earth. Thus we pray, *"Your kingdom come, Your will be done on earth as it is in Heaven."* What a wonderful privilege to bring God's future into the present, as N.T. Wright explains.

Our assignment is not to explain away why the Kingdom of God cannot come to earth, or why God's will cannot work here on earth. Our job is not to explain away the power of God because we do not see God's Kingdom everywhere. Our job is to lean into the agenda of the Kingdom, of the new creation. This is where history is going. We have the Holy Spirit in us in fullness. He's in our minds and hearts. It's no wonder that these dozen marks of new heavens and new earth throb within our breasts.

I want to support this magnetic pull we experience toward the new creation with three pictures. First, I do so by way of the picture of the inexhaustible Spirit flowing into a groaning creation, as seen in Ezekiel 47. While in Babylon Ezekiel is shown this picture in a vision: the temple, what we would now understand to be the people of God, has water flowing from below the threshold. To anticipate our conclusion, Jesus likens that water to the Holy Spirit (see John 7:37-39). Water of increasing measure, ankle-deep, knee-deep, waist-deep, and then water too-deep-to-cross pours from the temple. It flows into the Dead Sea, and remarkably that water becomes fresh. Further, everything will live where the river goes (see Ezek. 47:9). On both sides of the river there grows all kinds of trees for food. *"Their leaves will not wither nor their fruit fail, but they will bear fresh fruit every month, because the water for them flows from the sanctuary. Their fruit will be for food, and their leaves for healing"* (Ezek. 47:12).

Jesus uses this powerful Old Testament image to apply to the believers where living water flows from a person's innermost being bringing life wherever that person goes.

In 2008 in Southern California twenty-five people were killed on a MetroLink train that collided head-on with a freight train. In December of 2009 a new chief executive, John E. Fenton, was named. He said, "Everyone needs to realize that we don't move trains. We move people." His father was a pastor in Indiana and he once told his son, "People might forget what you say or do, but they will never forget how you make them feel."[6] Before he took over, ridership was dropping and morale was low. Now safety violations and injuries have decreased. On-time performance has risen. Ridership has increased by about 5,000 persons a day, and millions of dollars have been saved through changes in procedure. He provided service to a U2 concert in Anaheim and tapped into social media like Facebook and Twitter. Says Fenton, "I try to create an environment where people feel valued, where they can take ownership. Goodness is what motivates people."

Is it not possible to envision the turnaround at MetroLink to be life-giving water/spirit flowing where barrenness had existed? Oh to picture a river of life flowing from all of God's people. Oh to picture trees growing on both sides of the river producing all kinds of trees for food, with their leaves for healing. Pursue this imagery further, how does the Spirit issuing forth from the people of God supply food and healing? When the Spirit is flowing through us we are agents of love in helping others know sufficiency and healing. What a fantastic picture! The Spirit is inexhaustible. Fresh fruit every month, *"because the water for the trees flows from the sanctuary"* (Ezek. 47:12). Magnetic!

The second picture of the magnetic pull toward the new creation is the anticipation of the children of God being revealed (see Rom. 8:19). Now I want to introduce you to the modern-day "shepherd" to whom I referred at the beginning of this chapter. Dr. Steve Fitch heads Eden Reforestation Projects (edenprojects.org). His website shows land in Ethiopia five years prior (at the time of this writing) that was barren, and now, with trees planted, a whole ecology is developing: trees, brush, grasses. He anticipates on this spot that springs will soon emerge, and the people will not have to walk a number of kilometers in order to get nasty tasting water out of a lake. By the end of January 2012 Eden will have planted over 40 million trees in Ethiopia, Madagascar, and Haiti.

When Steve was revealed, when his life was unpacked, when his passion for serving God was unleashed and channeled, when he stepped into his calling, when the world got to know him (have him revealed), creation rejoiced. Here was a son of God who is participating in new creation/re-creation.

Creation is waiting with eager longing for the children of God to be revealed, or in the words of Dr. Todd of Compassion International, "to strive, to risk, and to capitalize on opportunities." Creation is looking forward to being set free from its bondage to decay. The children of God have obtained the *"freedom of the glory"* (Rom. 8:21). In becoming children of God we receive the birthright of freedom to participate in the glory—the great, substantive enterprise of God, and He is working and moving toward new creation in Christ. He is working toward, as we shall shortly see, all things reconciled to Himself, all things restored to their proper stations.

Creation desires to be free of its bondage to decay, obtaining the *"freedom of glory,"* the planet functioning as it ought. Creation was subjected to futility by the devil, but always in hope that it would be set free from its bondage to decay (see Rom. 8:20-21).

This modern-day shepherd, this modern-day Elzeard Bouffier, by the name of Steve Fitch, has been planting trees by the millions, and creation is being set free from decay. Like Bouffier nearly one hundred years earlier, Fitch plants trees, and a whole village system is nourished. He says the salaries from the jobs of planting trees allows the villagers to buy food, buy clothes, send their children to school, and go to the doctor when they are sick.

Two of the three powerful pictures contributing to the magnetic pull toward new creation are first, the inexhaustible river that Ezekiel shows bringing life to dead places as a promise of the inexhaustible resource of the Spirit available to us as we also lean into the agenda of new creation.

Second, the anticipation of the children of God being revealed, unpacked, introduced in their life-giving roles in the world, this anticipation contributes to the magnetic pull toward new creation.

The third picture of the magnetic pull toward new creation is the sparkling vision of all things reconciled to God, all things restored (see Col. 1:21; Acts 3:21). Let me attempt to illustrate this with a story I heard on National Public Radio.

> Richard Wagner's music is unofficially but effectively banned in Israel. Wagner was an anti-Semite. His family was close to Adolf Hitler. Beyond all that, his music was the soundtrack to the Holocaust; it was played at Nazi death camps. On July 25, 2011 in Bayreuth, Germany, the Israel Chamber Orchestra played Wagner's *Siegfried Idyll* with two of the composer's great-granddaughters sitting in the front row. Roberto Paternostro is the conductor of the Israel Chamber Orchestra.

> Paternostro said he loved Wagner's music as a student in Vienna. He was absolutely aware of what he was doing. He comes from a family of Holocaust survivors; his grandparents were dispatched to Auschwitz and eighty percent of his family were killed. Katharina Wagner, in charge of the Bayreuth Festival, is a friend of Paternostro. He asked about doing a concert there. The orchestra had a big discussion about the history of Richard Wagner, and then chose to play his music for the first time in their lives.

The conductor says that he's never seen an audience respond to a performance the way they did that night. He said, "I've conducted for more than twenty-five years all over the world, and I've never seen anything like it in my life. Everybody was so emotional—and many people came from Israel for the performance. After we finished the Wagner, there was such a great moment of silence, and then a standing ovation.

Why the response of the audience? Why the great moment of silence, and then a standing ovation? In a word, reconciliation. In a word, restoration. A chasm was bridged. A gulf was crossed. Drawn lines were erased. Grace was extended. Courage was demonstrated. The great moment of silence reflected the thoughtfulness of years, the consideration of the rationale for separation and distance and avoidance; the explosion of the standing ovation reflected the embrace of reconciliation, the thrill of walls coming down, the acknowledgment of beauty, the saluting of the courage of the Israeli conductor. Reconciliation and the restoration of all things is a dream deep in our hearts. On a summer's night in Bayreuth, Germany, the Israel Chamber Orchestra modeled all things being reconciled.

The new creation is magnetic. The picture of the inexhaustible Spirit making everything alive through God's people, the anticipation of the children of God taking on their true identity as "creation-blessers," and this powerful gravitational pull of anticipating all things being reconciled to God through Jesus Christ—these all thrill and captivate us.

The new creation includes untold numbers of shepherds who are planting acorns and trees. It includes orchestra directors, homemakers, students, business persons...you are likely one of them. Isaiah has listed the components by which we can understand the new heavens and the new earth. Jesus has started the new creation. Now, it remains for me to encourage you to "imagine that"!

ENDNOTES

1. Karen Mains, *Making Sunday Special* (Waco, TX: Word Books, 1987), 141f.

2. Ibid.

3. Ibid.

4. Scott Todd, "Poverty Is a Lie" *Mission Frontiers*, July-August 2011. http://www.missionfrontiers. org/issue/article/poverty-is-a-lie.

5. Ibid.

6. Dan Weikel, "Metrolink chief gets the railroad back on track," *Los Angeles Times,* August 6, 2011, A27.

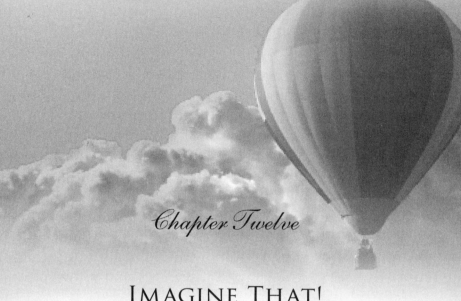

Chapter Twelve

IMAGINE THAT!

THE GREAT TRAGEDY OF ABORTION is that it disallows hope. We cannot hope for those fifty-four babies I reported at the outset of the book. This book seeks to overcome the abortion of hope by understanding that Jesus truly rules now; because of the cross and resurrection there is hope now. As I conclude this writing project I have a new and urgent interest in this matter of hope. Just a few months prior to completing this book I was diagnosed with an aggressive prostate cancer. Cancer, that's when the body is not as it should be; something is broken; something needs fixing. Cancer is a definition of a problem in the body, and it can serve as a metaphor for all manner of brokenness, from toxicity in Washington DC to intractable issues in the Middle East. Is there hope when the world is not yet as it should be?

Yes! This book makes this case; this book joins a growing volume of preachers, teachers, and authors who are declaring the good news of God, that the Kingdom has come in Jesus Christ, and therefore we have an ongoing assignment to join in declaring that good news, praying for God's Kingdom to come and His will to be done on earth as it is in Heaven, and working for this great vision.

I received two books while I was walking through my cancer journey. The first is a wonderful book by Pastor Dave Hess, a fellow graduate of Messiah College. He tells the gripping story of his journey with leukemia, a cancerous attack on the part of the body that manufactures blood. In the course of chemotherapy treatments his appendix ruptured. You can read the story in *Hope Beyond Reason* published by Destiny Image Publishers. Suffice it to say his book resounds with the message, "Yes, there is hope!" No matter the cancer or cancer-equivalent, there is hope! You and I have reason to believe that God can work when the world is not yet as it should be. Much of this book, *Soaring Hope*, is making the strong claim that Jesus is Lord now, He is ruling now, and we have reason to believe Him and His good news (see Mark 1:14-15).

A second book I received was on diet. I confess that when I received this book I was not particularly interested. However, two days after surgery to remove my prostate I received word from the pathology report that prostate cancer cells were found in the two lymph nodes that were removed that were adjacent to the prostate. That night I had a dream that I was in the kitchen where I grew up, and there were ants on the kitchen counter. I looked in the dishwasher (though there was no dishwasher in the kitchen where I grew up), and it looked like someone had thrown food scraps into the bottom of the dishwasher. There were ants there, and I immediately thought those food scraps were the source of the ants. Then, either at the end of the dream or immediately upon waking up I thought of the book on diet that I received, and I had this thought: perhaps food scraps in my body were the source of ants/cancer cells. So six days after surgery I began reading the book *The Hallelujah Diet* by George Malkmus. The stories of recovery from illness, including cancer, were remarkable. As I read further it was apparent that this book promoted not only a vegetarian but vegan diet. Following this diet sounded impossible. As I reflected further on the message of the book I thought, *Perhaps it's not all or nothing.* I began to think that there is something that I can do by way of my eating patterns to go along with my believing that there is hope that I can be healed of cancer.

I confess to loving potato chips, and especially crunchy potato chips. It is not unusual to remove my hands from the potato chip bag and observe that they are greasy and need to be washed. Simultaneously I have thought, I hope *I have sufficient substances inside to cleanse my system of the grease that surely is there.* Honestly, I remind myself of the fellow about ready to sleep, but who was very hungry for figs. He had a pile of them on his nightstand, but unfortunately the figs were bad. Fig after fig he had to discard because it was rotten or moldy. But because he was so terribly hungry, he finally shut off the light, and began to pop the figs into his mouth.

The diet book goes beyond believing there is hope, to outlining responses that I can and should make. It makes the case that the body has tremendous powers for self-healing if we give it the proper ingredients.

This book, *Soaring Hope*, calls us to believe that Jesus is Lord and that His Kingdom/rule has come in Him; this book also calls us to act based on that believing. God calls us to possess the land. As He said to Joshua, He says to us, "Take possession of the land I am giving you" (see Josh. 1:11). Indeed, imagine. Imagine the Lord's Prayer fulfilled. Imagine the will of God increasingly being done on earth as it is in Heaven. Imagine life as it ought to be.

Two of the clearest life patterns that identify to me the abortion of hope are sarcasm and passivity. This book seeks to be an antidote to those behaviors. Sarcasm reflects that one does not understand the good news of God, that His rule has come in Jesus Christ, and that we are to operate in that light, that is, we are to believe that message. I maintain that sarcasm is beneath the dignity of God's people. Sarcasm is aptly named, coming from the Greek word for flesh. Everywhere the Scriptures call us not to live according to the flesh. Sarcasm is anger not well-disguised by an attempt at humor. Sarcastic comments believe the worst about the motivations of others. "Yea, right!" Sarcasm taunts and sneers and cuts with caustic remarks. It jeers. It implies intent to hurt with mocking ridicule.

Sarcasm reflects the absence of deep confidence that Jesus is Lord, that His rule has come. Especially have God's people succumbed to sarcasm in political observations and engagement. We have sat in the seat of mockers and scoffers too long, listening to talk radio and online blogs. When we thoroughly believe the good news of God, we have neither the time nor the interest to be sarcastic. Rather we are believing that no matter the stage of cancer in the body, no matter the degree of toxicity in Washington DC, no matter the measure of difficulty between groups of people, Jews and Palestinians, for example, we believe there is hope for restoration and renewal. Nothing is too hard for God! Sarcasm suggests that persons do not understand the good news. Sarcasm believes that the news is bad. Sarcasm is wearying.

The second life pattern that identifies for me the abortion of hope is passivity. "Que sera, sera, whatever will be, will be. The future's not mine to see. Que sera, sera." The pervasive message of the Scriptures, however, is "possess the land." The story in Matthew 25 has slaves given talents, one given five talents, another given two talents, another given one talent. The master's clear intent is to grow the talents. This is what he meant by *"entrusting his property to them"* (see Matt. 25:14). Two of them doubled their talents, but one of them buried his talent, and to that one the most severe judgment in all the Bible is reserved for him: *"throw him into the outer darkness, where there will be weeping and gnashing of teeth"* (Matt. 25:30).

In your life and mine we are called away from passivity to the life of risk. Imagine possibilities! Imagine that! Imagine life as it ought to be.

Far from being sarcastic we are people who believe in God and hope in His work. We are people who understand that the night is far gone, the day is here. So it is we put on the armor of light; we live honorably as in the day (see Rom. 13:12-13). In the Lord we are light. We live as children of the light, for the fruit of the light is found in all that is good and right and true (see Eph. 5:8-9). Yes, we are children of the light and children of the day (see 1 Thess. 5:5). Because we are children of the light we make no provision for the flesh (see Rom. 13:14). Rather, the God of peace sanctifies us entirely (see 1 Thess. 5:23). With patience and perseverance we believe God's good news is for now. Now is the day of salvation! (See Second Corinthians 6:2.)

Let me tell you the story I referenced in Chapter One. South Africa lived with the reality of apartheid for many years. White people and people of color were separated: separate eating arrangements, separate bathrooms, separate travel arrangements. Horrific injustice was done to the people of color by whites who had all the power. However, some dreamed of what could be, of what life ought to be, and apartheid was dismantled. Then, a Truth and Reconciliation Committee was established whereby persons who had been wronged could have their voices heard. This story is told by John Roth in *Choosing Against War, A Christian View: A Love Stronger than Our Fears.*

> In the aftermath of apartheid's collapse in South Africa in 1994, the new government under Nelson Mandela established a Truth and Reconciliation Commission wose task it was to investigate specific acts of brutality committed in the name of apartheid and to seek some measure of resolution that would enable the country to move forward.

> At one meeting early in their work, the commission gathered to reach a verdict on a particularly painful case involving an elderly South African woman.

At the hearing, a group of white police officers, led by a Mr. van de Broek, admitted their personal responsibility in the death of her 18-year-old son. They acknowledged shooting the young man at point-blank range, setting his body on fire, and then partying around the fire until the body had been reduced to little more than ashes. Eight years later, van de Broek and his fellow officers had again intersected with the woman's life, this time to take her husband into captivity. And then, some time later, van de Broek had come knocking at her door once more. Rousing her from bed in the dead of night, he brought the woman to an isolated setting by a river where her husband lay tied to a pile of wood. As she watched, he and the officers doused the man with gasoline and then ignited a fire. The last words her husband spoke to her, in the midst of the blazing pyre, were "Forgive them."

Now at long last the time had come for justice to be served. Those involved had confessed their guilt, and the Commission turned to the woman for a final statement regarding her desire for an appropriate punishment.

"I want three things," the woman said calmly. "I want Mr. van de Broek to take me to the place where they burned my husband's body. I would like to gather up the dust and give him a decent burial.

"Second, Mr. van de Broek took all my family away from me and I still have a lot of love to give.

Twice a month, I would like for him to come to the ghetto and spend a day with me so I can be a mother to him.

"Third, I would like Mr. van de Broek to know that he is forgiven by God, and that I forgive him, too. And, I would like someone to come and lead me by the hand to where Mr. van de Broek is so that I can embrace him and he can know my forgiveness is real."

As the elderly woman made her way across the silent courtroom, van de Broek reportedly fainted, overcome by emotion. And then the silence was broken when someone began singing "Amazing Grace." Others soon picked up the words of the familiar hymn, so that finally the entire audience in the courtroom was joined in song.[1]

If this South African woman can show God's love after all that she had been through, then anything good is possible.

- Can you imagine, because Jesus is Lord, that Lou Gehrig's disease could be cured?

- Can you imagine, because Jesus is Lord, that we discover the cure for Huntington's disease?

- Can you imagine, because Jesus is Lord, that jobs and housing and health care and education are as good in Mexico as in the United States?

- Can you imagine, because Jesus is Lord, sophisticated training to help cultures in education and technology?

- Can you imagine, because Jesus is Lord, the arts helping children to master musical instruments and painting and sculpturing?

- Can you imagine, because Jesus is Lord, teaching literacy everywhere, and teaching writing skills to all?

- Can you imagine, because Jesus is Lord, girls growing into adulthood without sexual abuse, and boys growing into adulthood without sexual abuse?

- Can you imagine, because Jesus is Lord, helping young people to discover their dreams, and set on the journey to possess the land?

- Can you imagine, because Jesus is Lord, politics conducted with civility?

- Can you imagine, because Jesus is Lord, peace without fear in—you name the setting?

Is there any reason to spend our time explaining why young people ought not anticipate justice? Ought not anticipate God's will being done on earth? We need not carry as our deepest concern that these young people might become disappointed if they do not see the fullness of the Kingdom. Our forefathers in the faith were strong enough to handle disappointment with deep trust in God. The greater concern is that we do not live in faith, that we do not risk to possess the land, to multiply what God has given us. According to your faith be it unto you.

Now to Him who by the power at work within us is able to accomplish abundantly far more than all we can ask or imagine, to Him be glory in the church and in Christ Jesus to all generations, forever and ever. Amen (Ephesians 3:20-21).

ENDNOTE

1. John Roth, *Choosing Against War, A Christian View: A Love Stronger than Our Fears* (Intercourse, PA: Good Books, 2002), 62-63.

BIBLIOGRAPHY

Boyer, Paul. *When Time Shall Be No More.* Cambridge, MA: The Belknap Press of Harvard University Press, 1992.

Brother Andrew. *Light Force: A Stirring Account of the Church Caught in the Middle East Crossfire.* Grand Rapids, MI: Revell, 2004.

Christian History: Health Care and Hospitals in the Mission of the Church. Issue 101. Worcester, PA: Christian History Institute, 2011.

The Christians: Their First Two Thousand Years. Edmonton, AB, Canada: The Society to Explore and Record Christian History, 2011.

Dana and Mantey. *A Manual of the Greek New Testament*. Toronto: The Macmillan Company, 1955.

Dekker, Ted and Medearis, Carl. *Tea With Hezbollah*. New York: Doubleday Religion, 2010.

Ford, Desmond. *Crisis! A Commentary on the Book of Revelation*. Newcastle, CA: Desmond Ford Publications, 1982.

Ford, Desmond. *Daniel*. Nashville, TN: Southern Publishing Association, 1978.

Fudge, Edward William. *The Fire That Consumes: A Biblical and Historical Study of Final Punishment*. Houston: Providential Press, 1982.

Hess, Dave. *Hope Beyond Reason*. Shippensburg, PA: Destiny Image, 2008.

In Part: The Magazine for the Brethren in Christ Community in North America. Nappanee, IN: Evangel Press, Spring 2011.

Lewis, C.S. *The Last Battle*. New York: Macmillan Publishing Company, 1956.

Living Healthy, A Magazine for Blue Cross Blue Shield of Michigan Members. Spring 2010.

Mains, David and Karen. *Tales of the Kingdom*. Elgin, IL: David C. Cook Publishing Company, 1983.

Mains, Karen. *Making Sunday Special*. Waco, TX: Word Books, 1987.

Malkmus, George. *The Hallelujah Diet*. Shippensburg, PA: Destiny Image, 2006.

McLaren, Brian D. *Everything Must Change*. Nashville, TN: Thomas Nelson, 2007.

Roth, John. *Choosing Against War, A Christian View: A Love Stronger Than Our Fears*. Intercourse, PA: Good Books, 2002.

Stark, Rodney. *For the Glory of God*. Princeton, NJ: Princeton University Press, 2003.

Todd, Scott. "Poverty Is a Lie". Mission Frontiers, July-August 2011. (Go to www.missionfrontiers.org)

Vallotton, Kris. www.KVministries.com, search "eschatological core values.

Walsh, Patrick, and Worthington, Janet Farrar. *Guide to Surviving Prostate Cancer*. 2nd Ed. New York: Hachette Book Group, 2007.

Willard, Dallas. *The Divine Conspiracy*. New York: HarperSanFrancisco, 1997.

Wright, N.T. *Simply Christian: Why Christianity Makes Sense*. New York: HarperSanFrancisco, 2006.

About Lynn Thrush

Lynn Thrush has had the privilege of serving two congregations as pastor across thirty-three years, one church near Gettysburg, Pennsylvania, and the other in Southern California. The last fourth of these years has included adjunct teaching at Azusa Pacific University.

He is a graduate of Messiah College, BA; Asbury Theological Seminary, M.Div.; and Gordon-Conwell Theological Seminary, D.Min.

Anchored in the local community of faith, Lynn has been actively involved in the network of which he is part: his denomination, The Brethren in Christ Church, the pastors of the city where he ministers, Chino, and with friends of a wide variety of backgrounds.

He celebrates the faithfulness of God in his wife of thirty-seven years, their four adult children, grandchildren, and his experience of the energy of consistent hopefulness across the ministry decades. This book unpacks some of the rationale for living with expectation that includes both perseverance and exhilaration, and confidence that we reap harvest if we do not give up.

You can follow his writing, blogs, and communicate with him at LynnThrush.com.

IN THE RIGHT HANDS, THIS BOOK WILL CHANGE LIVES!

Most of the people who need this message will not be looking for this book. To change their lives, you need to put a copy of this book in their hands.

> *But others (seeds) fell into good ground, and brought forth fruit, some a hundred-fold, some sixty-fold, some thirty-fold* (Matthew 13:8).

Our ministry is constantly seeking methods to find the good ground, the people who need this anointed message to change their lives. Will you help us reach these people?

> *Remember this—a farmer who plants only a few seeds will get a small crop. But the one who plants generously will get a generous crop* (2 Corinthians 9:6).

EXTEND THIS MINISTRY BY SOWING
3 BOOKS, 5 BOOKS, 10 BOOKS, OR MORE TODAY, AND BECOME A LIFE CHANGER!

Thank you,

Don Nori Sr., Founder
Destiny Image
Since 1982